The Invisible Girl

The True Story of an Unheard Voice

TOREY HAYDEN

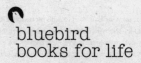

bluebird
books for life

First published 2021 by Bluebird
an imprint of Pan Macmillan
The Smithson, 6 Briset Street, London EC1M 5NR
EU representative: Macmillan Publishers Ireland Ltd, 1st Floor,
The Liffey Trust Centre, 117–126 Sheriff Street Upper,
Dublin 1, D01 YC43
Associated companies throughout the world
www.panmacmillan.com

ISBN 978-1-5098-6452-2

5 7 9 8 6 4

A CIP catalogue record for this book is available from the British Library.

Typeset in Charter ITC Std by Jouve (UK), Milton Keynes
Printed and bound by CPI Group (UK) Ltd, Croydon, CR0 4YY

Visit **www.panmacmillan.com** to read more about all our books
and to buy them. You will also find features, author interviews and
news of any author events, and you can sign up for e-newsletters
so that you're always first to hear about our new releases.

The Invisible Girl

chapter one

Chairs pulled into a tight circle, the children were taking turns at wearing sticky-backed labels on their foreheads. Each label had an emotion written on it, which the other children were acting out for the label-wearer to guess. The game's official name was 'Emotional Connection', a therapeutic game developed to help children recognize and express emotions. Amongst ourselves we called it the 'Silly Game', because it caused so much hilarity.

Carly was taking her turn, and her word was 'angry'. A curly haired seven-year-old with Down's syndrome, Carly danced around the circle so energetically that her label kept fluttering to the floor. This didn't matter much because Carly couldn't read, so she just picked it up and stuck it back on. The continual shrieks of 'You dropped it again!' added considerably to the overall chaos of six children trying to outdo each other's mimes of 'angry'.

When the door opened, I assumed it was someone from one of the offices, coming to ask us to be quieter. I hoped I could couch my apology in a gentle explanation that this was the last time we were scheduled to be here, and next week we'd be in the church hall.

Instead of opening properly, however, the door came ajar an inch or two, paused, then clicked shut again. The children didn't notice and carried on with the game. Perhaps it wasn't anyone after all. The weather was windy and the building draughty. Perhaps the door had not been closed properly and was moment-arily sucked off the latch by the wind before being pushed shut. I watched it a moment longer, but when nothing happened I turned my attention back to the children.

A few moments later, the door cracked open again. This time I saw an eye peering through. As soon as I looked, however, the door once again clicked shut. Time to investigate. The game paused briefly when the children saw me stand up, but I ges-tured for them to continue playing. I went to see what was going on. 'Hello?' I said, pushing the door fully open.

A girl stood in the dimly lit hallway. She looked to be in her early teens, a gangly, oval-faced girl with long, rumpled hair the colour of cardboard. She was dressed in a nondescript school uniform – white shirt, black cardigan, black trousers – but no tie, so I had no idea which school she attended.

'Are you Torey?' she asked.

'Yes.'

'Mrs Thomas said you would help me.'

Surprised, I raised my eyebrows. I hadn't talked to Meleri in weeks and my charity had not informed me that I'd be working with anyone new. The session I was running that day was the only work I was currently doing for Social Services. Known as an 'enrichment group', it was for special needs children of eight and under, who came from disadvantaged backgrounds. We met for an hour each week to work on social skills. I knew nothing about a teenage girl.

'What's your name?' I asked.

'Eloise.'

'Eloise what?'

She paused and gave a very slight shrug, as if she had to think about it, then replied, 'Eloise Jones.'

The momentary halt made me think she was reluctant to give her surname, so perhaps this was false. Even if it weren't, I wouldn't be much the wiser. Almost a third of the people in our part of Wales were surnamed Jones.

'There seems to have been a mix-up, because I don't have you on my schedule,' I said.

'Mrs Thomas told me you could help me,' she replied.

I glanced at my watch. 'This group doesn't end until 4.30. I'm not free before then.'

Her expression was hard to read. There was a vacancy to it that made me feel as if I was asking confusing questions.

'I have to go back in the room now,' I said, not needing to imagine the chaos taking place because I could hear it. I opened the door wide to let the kids know I was right there.

'Can I wait?' Eloise asked.

'It'll be at least twenty minutes.'

'That's okay.'

I didn't have a good reason to refuse her. We were just playing a game. Nothing private was taking place, so I said, 'Yes, that's fine,' and went back into the room to rejoin the children.

Eloise followed me in.

'Who's she?' one of the boys asked.

'Yes, who are you?' another one called across the room.

'This is a guest. Her name is Eloise. How do we greet a guest, Dylan? Do we shout "Who are you?" or do we say . . . ?'

'I know! I know! I know! Miss, I know!' This was eight-year-old Sallie, pushing her way out of the circle to run up to us. 'How do you do?' she said to Eloise. 'Hello, how is the weather?' Sallie's social graces might have carried slightly more weight if she hadn't had the word 'Disgust' plastered to her forehead.

There was a line of chairs along the side wall and I'd assumed Eloise would choose one of these until I'd finished with the group, but she came with me over to our circle and sat down with us.

The children were fascinated. Most of them were too shy to speak to her, but they danced back and forth, unwilling to return to the Silly Game. Dylan, who was seven, a sturdy boy with the physique of a miniature rugby player, had no such hesitancy. 'Who *are* you? Why are you here?'

I said, 'This is Eloise. She's visiting for today.'

'But *why*?'

This was hard to answer, given I didn't know myself. 'She's visiting, Dylan. That's enough information.'

'Where do you come from?' he asked her.

'Dylan, please sit down,' I said.

'Are you Welsh?' he asked.

'Dylan . . .'

'*T' siarad Cymraeg?*'

'Dylan . . .'

'I just want to know, is she going to be in this group? Are you going to be in this group? Because you're too big to be in this group. And we've got enough girls already.'

'*Stedd i lawr.*' I rose from my chair to ensure he did. He backed away and took his seat but continued to eye Eloise suspiciously.

Realizing that we weren't going to recapture the focus needed for the game, I decided to finish off with a story. I chose Judith Kerr's *The Tiger Who Came to Tea* for its engaging plot regarding a young girl who suddenly discovers a gentlemanly tiger at her door, and for the underlying emotions it provokes – in particular, excitement and anxiety. Who wouldn't be excited at the thought of hosting a real, live tiger in their house? Who wouldn't feel anxious about it?

I read the story and when I finished, I said, 'He was a very hungry tiger, wasn't he? What was the first thing he ate?'

'People,' Carly said. 'Tigers eat people.'

'But this tiger in the story didn't eat anyone, did he? What did he eat?'

'Tigers eat *people*,' Carly insisted.

'They bought him tiger food,' Owen said.

'At the end, they decided they would buy a tin of tiger food in case he visited again,' I replied. 'But they didn't give him any tiger food when he came to tea. What did they give him?'

Dylan huffed. 'There isn't such a thing as tiger food. You couldn't go to the shops and buy a tin of tiger food.'

'*What did they give him?*' I asked again.

'Everything!' Sallie replied. 'Everything they had for tea. And he drank everything too. All their tea and their orange juice and even all their water.'

'*Thank you,*' I said, relieved someone had been listening.

'I don't think it's possible to drink all the water in the tap,' Eloise said.

Surprised, I looked over.

Eloise continued, 'The tap is connected to the water mains. To drink the tap dry, he'd have to drink a whole reservoir of water. That isn't very realistic.'

The children were as taken aback as I was that Eloise had joined the conversation. They, I think, more because it had never occurred to them exactly how much water was in the tap in their kitchen. Me, because I hadn't expected her participation, to say nothing of the fact that this was a fictional story about a tiger sitting down at the table to share tea with a little girl and her mum, so not exactly a wildlife documentary.

'And he didn't even ask once to go to the toilet,' Sallie piped up.

When the children were finally away, I returned to Eloise, who had remained in her chair in the circle. I took an adjacent chair. 'So, tell me, how can I help you?'

'I have to get back to my foster home in Moelfre.'

Perplexed by the request, I said, 'That's a long way from here.' Given that I did nothing even faintly related to transporting children to different places, I asked, 'Can you explain a bit about this, please?'

Eloise looked away and gave a frustrated little huff, the kind teenagers give when adults are being dim. She huffed again, looked back. 'There's been, like, this big misunderstanding. Over the ring. I didn't take it. For real, I didn't, but Olivia got angry, so I got moved from the Powells' to this other place and I hate it. Because it was all a big mistake. Olivia texted me and said she was sorry. See, this boy Sam gave it to me. The ring, I mean. But it belongs to Olivia, and he took it, but she understands now that I didn't take it. So I need to get it back to her or I'll be in such big trouble.'

I was absolutely lost. I knew nothing about this drama nor any of the characters in it. 'Let's back up a minute. You say Mrs Thomas told you *I* could help you?'

Eloise nodded. 'She said you write books. And you help people.'

'Did she explain how I can help?'

Another frustrated huff, less patient this time. '*I* don't know. Mrs Thomas just said. I told her I needed to get the ring back to Olivia, and Mrs Thomas said you could help me because you write books. So, please. That's why I came here. Please?'

I could make no sense of any of this. A completely random girl shows up and wants me to aid her in getting back to her old foster home so that she can return a piece of jewellery? It was like some weird Social Services version of *The Lord of the Rings*.

'Where do you go to school?' I asked.

'This has nothing to do with school,' Eloise replied.

I regarded her.

When she realized I wasn't going further with the conversation until she'd answered, she said, 'Ysgol Dafydd Morgan,' with an irritated sigh. I recognized it as a secondary school in a coastal town more than ten miles away.

'You wouldn't be able to get over here so quickly from Dafydd Morgan.'

Eloise bulged her eyes to indicate how irritating I was being. 'I took the bus.'

'But you skived?' I replied.

She shook her head. 'No.'

'You had permission to leave early?' I asked sceptically.

Her voice became piteous. 'Come *on*. *Please?*'

I paused a moment to think, and silence slid in around us.

Eloise was staring at her lap when I raised my head, giving me a moment to study her. She was a plain girl. Her features were flat, her eyes a nondescript bluish-grey, her mouth small and thin-lipped. Long, wavy brown hair, which should have been tied back for school, hung over her shoulders. I could imagine her as one of those kids who slipped out of school unnoticed, one of those kids living around the edges of life because they barely stood out from the background.

'May I see the ring?' I asked, mostly to verify that there actually was one.

Eloise had a small black handbag on a shoulder strap and she pulled it onto her lap and opened it. An initial root through it didn't turn up the ring, which immediately made me suspicious that she hadn't been telling me the whole story.

Eloise seemed to sense my disbelief, because she became visibly distressed when she couldn't find it. Opening the bag wider, she began to search again.

'Hold on,' I said, 'where did you get all that?' Among the things in the bag I could see several packages of paracetamol.

Not replying, she quickly stuffed the boxes down into the depths, pulling items over them.

'No, hold on. Let me see those, please,' I said, and reached out. Eloise resisted, pulling the bag around her body.

'Give me your handbag, please.'

'It's mine.'

'Yes, I know, but give it to me, please.'

A long moment passed between us, Eloise with the handbag gripped to her chest. We locked eyes.

'Give it here, please,' I said again.

Finally a sigh and she let go.

I took the handbag into my lap and opened it. One, two, three, four, five boxes of paracetamol, sixteen tablets in each of them. Sales of these tablets were restricted to a total purchase of thirty-two tablets specifically to reduce the chances of a person dying in a case of overdose. Acquiring five boxes meant careful planning, and this spoke to me of one thing only: suicide.

'What's this about?' I asked.

'It's just headache medicine.'

'There are too many here for a headache.'

'I get migraines.'

'This is too much medicine, even for migraines.'

Despair touched her features. 'It's not what it looks like,' she said.

'This is too much medicine to have all at once.'

Her mouth pulled down. Her chin quivered.

'Something's gone very wrong, hasn't it?'

She nodded.

'Can you tell me about it?'

She shook her head.

'I'm happy to help you, if I can, but I need to understand what's going on.'

Eloise shook her head again.

'What can I do to help?' I asked.

'Please just take me to Moelfre.'

'I'm not able to do that. I'll take you back to school, if you like. Or I'll take you to Mrs Thomas's office.'

'No, I want to go home.'

'I'm confused,' I said. 'Moelfre is well up the vale and you're attending Ysgol Dafydd Morgan. That's twenty miles in the other direction, so I'm thinking Moelfre isn't home.'

'Yes, it is. I need you to take me there.'

'Let me phone Mrs Thomas and get the details. In the meantime, let's leave these here.' I took hold of the boxes of paracetamol.

'Can't you *understand*?' Eloise wailed. '*I need to get back to Olivia. I need to bring her the ring!*' She flapped her hands in a frantic spasm, almost as if she was going to hit herself, but she didn't. Crossing her arms tightly across her chest, she clamped her hands on her shoulders and rocked forward.

I felt a twinge of alarm. I didn't know anything about this girl at all, but I sensed self-harm in her behaviour and far more serious problems than simply getting a ring back to someone.

Touching her shoulder, I said, 'I can see you really want to do that. But just for now, it's important to me that you stay safe. I can tell something is wrong and you're feeling very unhappy. So let me help you. Let me start by keeping hold of these for the moment. And let me talk to Mrs Thomas. Then I promise I will help you sort out the matter of your ring and Olivia. I promise.'

The tension eased a little. Eloise snuffled and covered her face with one hand. I handed her a couple of tissues. Two or three minutes passed while she recomposed herself. Finally she nodded. 'Okay.'

'Good. Good girl.' Putting my arm around her shoulder, I gave her a little squeeze.

'I'm sorry,' she said. 'I didn't mean to get so upset.'

'That's all right.'

She nodded. 'Can I use the toilet?'

'Yes, of course.'

She rose from the chair and reached across me for her bag. I kept my hand on it. 'No, leave all this here, please. The toilet is just down the hall to the right.'

Without further protest, Eloise left.

I put the boxes of paracetamol in my own handbag. Collecting together all the materials I'd brought for the enrichment group, I put them into my satchel and then tidied up the room.

For five minutes or so I didn't think much about Eloise's

absence, but as the minutes continued to pass a sense of fore-boding came over me. Taking her handbag along with my own things, I went out and closed and locked the door behind me.

There were separate toilets for men and women, but only one of each. Both doors were closed but neither appeared occupied. I knocked at the door to the women's. When there was no answer, I pushed it open. Empty. I knocked at the door of the men's and again pushed it open when there was no answer. Empty.

Horrified, I looked up and down the hallway. Nothing. Eloise was gone.

chapter two

Panic rose in my throat. Walking down the hall, I peered into offices as I went, even though it seemed highly unlikely she'd go into one of those rooms. The building was a modern single-storey structure that wasn't very large, so it took me only a few minutes to reach the back entrance. I opened the door and looked out. Immediately behind the building was a drab concrete area and then a high chain-link fence, separating us from a derelict plot beyond. Closing the door, I went back through the building to the front and looked out there. No one could be seen anywhere. Absolutely no one.

Our building was on a narrow, dead-end street that ran alongside the river. There was nothing on the opposite side of the street except the river itself. A path popular with dog walkers was on that side, but the tide was in, so the river was wide and dark. No one walked that side of the road when the tide was in because the path was always muddy.

Next door was a modern prefab building where they did something with tyres. Beyond our cul-de-sac there were only fields. These were not nice, green farm fields but a rough, post-industrial landscape of broken concrete and rusting metal that nature was slowly reclaiming.

The only direction Eloise could have gone was to the left, past the tyre place and on towards the town. I had a good view of the street going in that direction and I could see no one. There was only one thing left to do: phone Meleri.

Meleri Thomas was one of the social workers with the local council. We'd first met several years earlier, when I was very newly arrived in Wales from the United States. On that occasion, she and I were both guests on a television programme. Everything was so overwhelmingly new to me at that point that I probably wouldn't have remembered Meleri beyond the fact that I mistook her for the popular TV chef Nigella Lawson. However, Meleri proved to be in that 'once met, never forgotten' category, as much for her flamboyant personality and love of brightly coloured, figure-hugging clothes as for her resemblance to a celebrity. She definitely was not your average social worker.

We next met at a conference, and it was then we discovered that we both lived in the same part of North Wales. The rest, as they say, is history. Meleri and I worked on and off together for several years.

The British system is quite unique in its integration of charitable organizations and government programmes. In areas such as health, education and welfare, there are many instances of the government providing infrastructure and supplemental funding for programmes which are then run in large part by charities. For example, for a person diagnosed with cancer, medical treatment comes from the National Health Service, but closely allied charities provide crucial assistance ranging from practical help, such as financial advice or transport to and from the hospital, to emotional support, to specialized nursing such as pain management or end-of-life care.

When I moved to the UK I was unable to work as a teacher or psychologist because my immigration visa restricted my employment to writing. By the time I was eligible for employment in these fields I was raising a young family and didn't want full-time work. Consequently, becoming part of the charitable system worked well for me. There were a number of organizations where I could make use of my background in special education and psychology. I spent most of my time working with one of the larger children's charities, providing one-to-one counselling and leading enrichment groups for children coming from deprived or abusive backgrounds. I also regularly contributed to workshops and training sessions for teachers and other allied workers on topics such as child abuse and autism. Because it was Meleri who had first charmed me into working locally, I ended up doing most of my work within the foster care system, and this was time well spent because many of these children had virtually no access to therapeutic support otherwise. Most of them came to me via a referral from Meleri, so Eloise's saying Mrs Thomas had sent her was plausible, although I would not have expected Meleri to do so without giving me a heads-up first.

*

Torey Hayden

'*Eloise?*' Meleri said in shock. 'There? With you?'

Fourteen-year-old Eloise had run away from her foster home several days earlier. No one, including Meleri, had seen her in that time. Finding this out I felt an even deeper sense of alarm, given the packages of paracetamol. I also felt distressed realizing Eloise had made such a special effort to find me and I had inadvertently scared her off. There was no time, however, for ruminating over what might have been done better, because all that mattered at that moment was finding her.

Meleri filled me in on Eloise's background, an all-too-common litany of family dysfunction, addiction and abuse, interspersed with Social Services intervention and stints in foster care. She was one of three children, all with different fathers. Her brother, two years younger, had been so violently assaulted that he suffered permanent brain damage and subsequently died of a seizure. Eloise, aged four, came into the system at this point, along with her sister, Evie. The girls went to separate foster homes, and some time later, parental rights for Evie were terminated and she was cleared for adoption.

For reasons not clear to me, Eloise was not released for adoption at the same time as Evie. Instead, she ended up going back to her mother when she was six. Things appeared to go well. Eloise attended school regularly, was clean and cared for, and seemed settled. However, when Eloise was nine, the mother's boyfriend, a man named Darren, was arrested for posting pornographic photos of Eloise online. Police investigation showed that photos and videos of Eloise had been appearing online for a couple of years and Eloise's mother as well as her boyfriend

16

had been involved. The mother's parental rights were terminated at this point.

Understandably, Eloise was showing signs of troubled behaviour by this point, and was placed in a therapeutic foster home. She responded well and made reasonable progress. Unfortunately, therapeutic foster homes are, by their nature, short-term stays, so after nine months Eloise was moved on to a new foster home. Again, she settled without too much difficulty. Then her paternal grandmother appeared. Up to this point Eloise's father had played almost no role in her life because he had been in and out of prison on drug-related charges. The grandmother said he was now out, clean, working steadily, and living with her. The family wanted to rebuild their relationship with Eloise and give her a home.

This was good news to Social Services, who did their best to keep children with their own families whenever possible. Unfortunately, Eloise's father and grandmother lived in an adjacent county, which meant both a different jurisdiction for Social Services and little opportunity for Eloise to spend time with them before being allowed to go to live with them. Meleri said she'd felt at the time that this was a questionable decision, not only because Eloise was settled well in her foster home, but because the father and grandmother lived in a deeply rural inland community where Welsh was spoken as a first language. This meant the local school would be conducted in Welsh with English as the second language, whereas Eloise, whose mother was English, was not yet proficient at Welsh. Meleri feared that, after such a disruptive childhood, expecting Eloise to adapt to a new language as well as a new home and new family was too big an ask. Meleri was overruled, however, and Eloise went.

And Eloise came back. The arrangement broke down within a few months when the father's drug problems recurred and the grandmother couldn't cope with Eloise's complex behavioural needs.

This was the point, aged thirteen, that Eloise was placed in Moelfre with the Powell family, who'd had many years' experience of fostering. Their household included a daughter, Heddwen, who was sixteen at this point, and son, Rhys, nineteen, who was away at university, as well as two long-term foster children. There was no one named Olivia.

Both Heddwen and her brother had grown up with foster children coming and going, and as a consequence they were skilled at making the newcomers feel welcome. Meleri said that Eloise had had problems settling in, complicated by the fact that she got her first period soon after she'd arrived and was completely unprepared for it. Heddwen had empathized with her, reassuring Eloise by sharing her own experiences of this milestone, and tried to be especially supportive of her in these early days. Unfortunately, according to Meleri, Eloise interpreted Heddwen's kindness as signs of a deeper connection. Infatuation soon followed.

Eloise started to follow Heddwen around the house and wanted to be with her constantly. She attempted to hold Heddwen's hand, cling to her physically, and cuddle up close on the sofa whenever Heddwen sat down. Heddwen was uncomfortable with the nature of Eloise's physical contact and didn't want

Eloise to touch her. Then, Eloise began to show jealousy whenever Heddwen wanted to spend time with other people, and was particularly difficult when Heddwen had her friends over to the house. Despite efforts to discourage Eloise's attentions, Heddwen increasingly found she was unable to go about normal activities. Things came to a head one Saturday afternoon when Heddwen went out with her boyfriend. In a fit of jealous rage, Eloise took scissors and destroyed several articles of Heddwen's clothing. The Powells' had had enough. They requested that Eloise be moved to a different foster home.

Her current placement was in one of the large coastal towns, more than thirty miles from Moelfre. This distance had not completely deterred Eloise, however. She still managed to turn up on several occasions in the Powells' front garden to watch the house and wait for Heddwen to come out, and she'd resisted efforts to help her settle into her new foster home. Twice she had run away; twice the police had found her. This was the third time, and Eloise had been missing from home for almost a week.

'How on earth did she think to come to me?' I asked.

'I can only suppose it's because of what I said,' Meleri replied. 'She'd had a bad turn after the last time she was caught at the Powells'. I went to get her from the police station – she was crying and saying how horrible we all were for not letting her be with Heddwen, and *all* she could focus on was getting back there. I was trying to explain that I couldn't let her return to the Powells', how this thing with Heddwen had to stop because it wasn't real. Her *feelings* were real, but the relationship wasn't real, because Heddwen didn't reciprocate. For all my explanation, she just wouldn't let go of the idea that she wanted to be with Heddwen. She cried and cried and cried. Suicide kept coming into the conversation, and she kept going on about how none of us were helping her . . . I was desperately trying to think of something to distract her, to get her off that train of thought, because she was in so much distress . . . I said something like maybe she could talk to you sometime, maybe you could help.' Meleri paused. 'I may have egged the pudding a bit, because I said how you were famous and very good at solving problems. Her mind was so one-track at that moment, so I was just saying anything I thought might work. But it was only a mention. I never followed up on it. As you know, because you and I've never talked about her.'

'Wow,' I said. 'So from that, she got here?'

'Apparently. But I have no idea how she found out where you were. I have no idea how she actually got to you. And I have no idea what we do next.'

chapter three

The boxes of paracetamol were still sitting on the chair beside me when I came off the phone with Meleri. I had no doubt that Eloise had genuinely intended to take them if she couldn't get resolution to her problem with Heddwen, and, given how meticulously she had tracked me down, I was quite certain that she was more than capable of laying the groundwork for a successful suicide.

I particularly hated that she had chosen paracetamol, because it would be easy for her to get it again, and most people don't realize what a nasty drug it is in overdose. It doesn't kill outright. Instead, as the body tries to break it down, it creates a by-product that causes liver failure, which means the person may wake up from the overdose with a change of heart, hoping to move forward, but still die several days later if the overdose has not been appropriately treated. This had happened with a young person I'd worked with. This girl had overdosed in a moment of acute despair. Fortunately, she was found, and the friend who found her had made her vomit, thinking this was the best way to get the poison out of her body, and then, instead of getting medical help, had let her sleep it off. The next day she woke up grateful to still be alive, and focused on getting the help she needed, yet she died five days later because too much of the paracetamol had been metabolized, leaving her liver damaged. I had been absolutely gutted by the news.

So what would happen to Eloise? What were we going to do? What could we do? None of us knew where she was or how to get hold of her. I don't think I've ever felt so helpless.

Coming off the phone with Meleri, I made one last attempt at finding Eloise locally. I went down to the road and looked carefully over the surrounding area. The day was overcast with high, ribboned clouds. The trees had been nipped here and there with frost but were still mostly green, their leaves looking tired.

I saw no one. Because the road was a dead end, even traffic was absent. The tyre place next door was a small, independent company, and never very busy. Now it looked dead. No cars in the car park. No lights on. The river opposite was black and slow-moving. I stood a few moments longer, willing Eloise to be there somewhere, maybe waiting for a bus or walking along the road, but there was nothing.

Returning to the room, I packed up my things and all the boxes of paracetamol, moved chairs back into their places, turned out the lights and left.

Normally I worked quite close to home, but the enrichment group was being held in one of the small villages along the Welsh–English border. The charity hadn't been able to find anyone else to run it; though it was an hour away from where I lived, it was held only once a week, and I enjoyed the drive.

Eschewing the busy A55, I always took the small back roads, which were slower but more direct, and wound their way through the astonishingly picturesque Welsh countryside.

On this occasion, all I could think of was Eloise as I drove. Seeing the high hedgerows and rural bus stops, I wondered how on earth Eloise had managed to figure out how to get from her home on the coast to the small village. I felt bad that she had made such an effort and I'd not responded with the sensitivity she needed.

The drawback to my position as a volunteer was that I was never considered to be on the front line. Indeed, in most instances, I was not in the hierarchy at all. Consequently, when Eloise was finally located and returned to her foster home, no one told me. This wasn't Meleri's fault. She was off work that week and a different social worker was handling her cases, and this lady didn't know about my connection. When Meleri returned and caught up on her work, she did phone and said that Eloise had already been moved to a new foster home in hopes it would be a better fit and deter her from running away. She was now in one of the villages on the western edge of the county, as far from the Powells as Social Services could manage to place her without moving her out of the district altogether.

I was pleased to hear this, because it meant Eloise was much closer to me geographically, so I said I would be happy to work with her, if Meleri thought that would be helpful. Unfortunately, however, the move meant Eloise was no longer on Meleri's caseload, so if I was to become involved, I needed to wait until the new social worker put in a request to my charity for my services, and there was no guaranteeing when that would happen or, indeed, if it would happen. Such is the way things work in an imperfect world.

Life moved on, as it inevitably does. September became October. The trees changed. The autumn gales started. October ended, and in came November, regarded as the first month of winter in the Celtic countries. The last of the autumn colour still clung to a few trees, but mostly drifted at the edges of roads, brown and gold leaves scattering in the slight breeze. The days shortened and turned dull and gloomy.

Home for me was a small hill farm a thousand feet up on the Hiraethog moor. We were on the west side, overlooking the mountains of Snowdonia, where the untamed land began to slowly drift back into cultivated farmland. As both my husband and I had other jobs, we weren't full-time farmers, but we liked the country lifestyle, and raised sheep and a few cattle, plus an assortment of poultry.

This particular autumn, we had a motherless Jersey calf named Gerald. Gerald had only recently come to us, and caring for him mostly involved filling a recycled two-litre Coke bottle with calf replacement milk, screwing on a rubber teat with the proportions of a sex toy, and spending half an hour trying to get Gerald to open his mouth enough to accept it. Gerald was not easily convinced of the value in doing this. He weighed almost as much as I did and could clamp his mouth shut very tightly, so mealtimes were a messy affair. I always suited up in wellies, waterproof jacket and trousers before getting down in the straw with him to wrestle the rubber teat into his mouth.

On this particular day, I had been away from home and only returned as dusk was falling. My husband was already home by the time I got there, and he and our daughter were in the kitchen making the evening meal. As much as I did not feel like wrangling calves at that moment, I knew it was my turn, so I changed clothes and pulled on my waterproofs. I crossed the yard, the full Coke bottle under my arm. The loose box had a typical stable door. Normally, we latched the lower half to keep Gerald in, and left the upper half open to let the stink out, because calves are quite smelly things in a confined area. It was virtually dark, so I flipped on the light, greeted Gerald and let myself in, shutting the lower half of the door behind me and latching it. As I knelt down in the straw beside Gerald, I wasn't thinking about anything much except the task at hand.

After a week of having the teat forced between his lips, it had slowly dawned on Gerald that the contents of the bottle were rather nice. So after a messy start, he tentatively began to suck. Just as I was rejoicing in this small miracle, a shape loomed unexpectedly at the stable door. Both Gerald and I startled and milk went everywhere.

'Hi,' came the shy voice. There stood Eloise.

I was so surprised to see her, I was momentarily speechless.

She looked frightened, as if it had been me who had startled her.

'Whatever are you doing here?' I asked.

Torey Hayden

There was a long pause, and then she said, 'Mrs Thomas told me you're an author. I've seen your books.'

'How did you find me?'

Lips slightly parted, eyes wide, her expression remained almost blank. She shrugged slightly. In just that moment, Eloise looked as if she really didn't know, as if she had been somehow magicked out of her life and into mine.

'Come inside,' I said. 'It's starting to rain again.'

She shook her head. 'I'm scared of that.' She gestured towards Gerald.

'He won't hurt you. He's just little.'

'I don't want him to bite me.'

'He's a calf. He won't bite.'

She shook her head again. 'I'm scared of animals.'

Again, the long pause. We looked at each other, both of us speechless.

'I want you to help me,' she said at last. 'Like you do the kids in your book. I want to be in your class.'

'I'm not a teacher these days, I'm afraid.'

'But Mrs Thomas said you would help me. I want that.'

I smiled. 'Yes, and I'm sure we can sort something out. But we need to talk to your social worker first.'

Eloise made a face.

'We also need to agree on a few rules first. For example, you need to go to school regularly. I'm not a substitute for attending school. Another thing, you need to promise me you won't keep running away, because I can't help you if I don't know where you are.'

'I haven't run away.'

'You're still with the Jenkinses?'

'Yes.'

'So how did you get clear up here?'

'Bus.' Her tone implied I was being a bit thick for not knowing this.

'There are no buses on our lane.'

Eloise shrugged. 'I got off at the village. I walked from there.'

'Yes, well, this is the thing. It's after dark. You're wearing a black coat and black trousers. And we're in the middle of nowhere. It isn't safe to do that for all sorts of reasons. I'm glad to know you are still with the Jenkinses, but they'll be worried about where you are at this time of day, and it's important to me that I know you are safe. So if I'm going to help you, we will need to arrange a time and place. I don't want you just turning up.'

'Don't you want to see me?'

'That's not the point, Eloise. I'm happy to see you, and I'm not cross. What I'm saying is that it's not safe the way you've done it. I don't want you walking alone along unlit roads at dusk, especially when you are dressed in dark clothing. We need to do it a different way.'

'I didn't know another way to get to talk to you. Nobody remembers that Mrs Thomas said I could see you.'

I smiled. 'I understand. But from here on, we want to stick to ways that are safe and legal and won't get anyone run down on the road. Yes?'

She gave a one-shouldered shrug.

At that moment, Gerald wobbled to his legs and stumbled

around behind me. He nuzzled my hair, took a few more steps and then began a massive pee.

Eloise gasped in horror. 'That is so gross!' she squealed, but there was laughter in her voice. 'And you're just sitting there. He's practically peeing on you!' She was clearly finding this funny. 'It's making splatters on your rain jacket. He's close enough that pee is getting on you.'

'That's a calf for you,' I said, as I rose to my feet. 'And why I'm wearing waterproofs. Fortunately, the rain will wash everything off when I go outside.'

'Do you like this?' she asked, waving a hand out in an arc. 'Living out here like this?'

'Yes, I do.'

'I wouldn't. Everything here is gross and scares me.'

Buses going to the nearby village were few and far between, so I told her I would drive her home. I'd expected this would be a good time to talk, to get to know her just a little bit better, and to lay out plans for doing something together. For the first fifteen minutes or so, however, we travelled in complete silence. While I had so many things in my head I wanted to say, being with Eloise was akin to being with a wild animal that has unexpectedly come up to you. It was clear she wanted to be with me, but I still had the sense that the slightest wrong move on my part, however innocent, could spoil things. So when the silence settled in between us, I was hesitant to break it.

'Can I play your radio?' she asked.

'Yes, of course.'

She leaned forward to turn it on. Prokofiev burst forth unexpectedly loudly and Eloise jerked back in surprise. 'What's *that*?' she asked, her voice suspicious at the mincing sounds of the Montagues and Capulets, but before I could answer she started punching buttons until she found the radio station she wanted. We drove on, listening to Madonna.

'How would you like me to help you?' I asked.

Eloise didn't answer.

'When you set out to come find me this afternoon – because that was quite a journey you made – what were you hoping I could do?'

'I don't know.'

Silence.

'I don't know,' she said again. I could hear tears behind her words.

'That's okay,' I said. 'I was just asking.'

A long silence followed.

'You helped those other children . . . the ones in your book. And I want you to help me like that . . .'

'Can you tell me what you'd like me to help with?'

'I don't know.'

Silence.

'When Mrs Thomas suggested you talk to me, what were you talking about, do you remember? What was happening that made Mrs Thomas suggest me?'

A very long silence followed then, so long that I feared I was going to arrive at her address before she answered. She must have thought this too, because she began to gather her things together in preparation for getting out of the car.

'I need to see Olivia,' she said, just as I pulled up outside her house. 'Mrs Thomas won't let me. No one will let me. They said I have to forget her, but I can't. I want you to help me get back with her.'

I was still formulating my response when she opened the door abruptly and got out. She looked over at me. 'I don't want to live. No joking. If I can't be with Olivia then I don't want to live.' And she turned and left.

chapter four

Eloise's new caseworker was a lady named Sue Pugh, and absolutely everyone who spoke about her always used both names. Sue-Pugh. An older lady, sturdily built, with short, grey hair that was always a bit sticky-outy, as if she'd just been bear-hugged by an actual bear, Sue-Pugh came from that no-nonsense, tough love, pull-your-socks-up brigade of middle-class ladies who'd been sent off to boarding school at eight and had loved every moment. She'd been in social work for almost thirty years and, I suspect, had pretty much seen it all. Meleri still wore her heart on her sleeve some days, but I doubt this was ever a problem with Sue-Pugh.

I found her a bit intimidating, because I got the sense from Sue-Pugh that she thought the kinds of things I did, such as the enrichment groups, were airy-fairy American confections that I'd brought with me to ruin the British stiff upper lip. I was never 100 per cent sure if her comments on things like this were genuine brusqueness or simply a very dry sense of humour. Consequently, I was always hesitant to interact with her, and so

I put off the phone call regarding Eloise until I had all the permissions from my charity in place.

I needn't have worried. Sue-Pugh was more than happy for me to work with Eloise on a one-to-one basis. The only prerequisite, she said, was that I needed to see Eloise in the village where her foster home was, because they were enforcing her physical distance from Moelfre and the Powell family. Eloise was not allowed to leave the village, Sue-Pugh explained. I didn't mention that Eloise had already visited me on the moors.

The village hall was a flat-roofed, single-storey building. I was assigned one of the small side rooms at the back of the building to work with Eloise. I had no idea what purpose the room may have had in days gone by, because it was much too small to be a classroom, yet too large to be a storage closet. Painted stark white, it had a single small window in the end wall that was so high up you couldn't see out. A white haze over the glass gave testament to the fact that it hadn't been cleaned in a very long time, as did the cobwebs. Along one wall was a line of nine black plastic chairs, and at the very end an odd wooden table. Also painted white, it was about a metre square and had unusually long legs, making the tabletop come neck high if you used one of the chairs in the room to sit down at it.

Dismayed at how uncongenial the room was, I walked through the building to see if there might be some other more comfortable place. Everywhere had the cool dankness of a building not in use every day. Unable to find anywhere better, I returned to find Eloise had already arrived.

'We haven't got much here, I'm afraid,' I said, gesturing to the weird table and the line of chairs against the wall.

Eloise just stood.

'How would you like to do this? Shall we pull the chairs into a circle?'

'Why? There's just you and me,' she replied. Her tone wasn't challenging. If anything, she sounded weary.

'Okay, well, shall we use the table then? It's rather high, but we could put the chairs this way.' I set two chairs at the table and then sat.

Eloise continued standing.

I looked up at her. Black wool coat, long grey scarf, school uniform, thick tights, standard school shoes. Her long hair was tied back in a low ponytail.

'You might be more comfortable if you remove your coat. There are hooks just outside the door.'

'It's too cold in here.'

'It is cold. I'll try to bring a heater next week.'

'Am I meeting you next week?' she asked, her expression confused.

'Yes, that's the plan. You and I will meet each Thursday afternoon and see if we can sort things out for you.'

Eloise stood there, her expression blank. It unnerved me, because she behaved almost as if she didn't know who I was or why I might be there.

Silence.

Finally Eloise dropped her school things onto one of the chairs against the wall. She didn't remove her coat, but she unbuttoned it and loosened her scarf. A few more moments passed and at last Eloise sat down at the table. The bewildered expression remained on her face.

Normally when I work one to one, I start by asking the child to tell me in their own words what they see are the problems that have brought them to me. This gives me an idea of the amount of insight they have into their issues, as well as which problems are foremost in their mind.

'I can tell you really want to change things,' I started. 'It took resourcefulness to find where I was when I was teaching the enrichment group, and then again to get all the way up to my farm by yourself. That took courage. I was impressed by how much you want to make changes. So let's see what we can do together. How can I help?'

'What do you mean?' she asked.

'You want me to help you. Can you tell me the things you'd like me to help you with?'

Eloise said nothing. She sighed, lowered her head. Then she leaned far forward and put her head right down on the table-top, forehead against the wood. 'Olivia,' she said at last, without sitting up.

'Olivia? Okay, a good place to start is by telling me a little more about Olivia.'

Eloise shrugged, still leaned forward against the tabletop. 'What do you want to know?'

'For one thing, who she is.'

'*Olivia.*'

'Okay, but I'm a bit confused. When you first came to see me at the enrichment group, you said the problem was that you needed to get back to see Olivia. You said you had her ring, that you'd got somehow, and you needed to take it back to Olivia. You wanted me to help. Is that right?'

Eloise didn't say anything.

'When I talk to Sue-Pugh about your problems, she tells me the issue is with the Powell family, specifically with Heddwen Powell. Perhaps you could tell me more about Olivia and how she fits into this.'

Eloise finally straightened back up. Briefly she looked over at me and then away.

'What's Olivia's last name?'

No reply.

I let the question hang in the air for several moments.

'I just want you to help me get back there,' Eloise finally said. 'I don't like it here. I want to go back to the Powells. I promise I'll do everything right. I won't get in trouble. I promise that. You have my word. So that's all you have to do. That's all I want you to do.'

'Unfortunately, that's not in my power.'

Eloise grimaced. 'Then I might as well not bother.'

'Hold on. You've bothered a lot up until now,' I said. 'So let's not give up at the first hurdle. Let's talk things through, because maybe I can help in other ways.'

'Talking never helps anything,' she replied grimly.

'Just tell me about Olivia. Forget all the rest of it. You have Olivia's ring. You want to give it back to her. What's the story behind this? Who is Olivia?'

Eloise raised her shoulders as if to shrug but then lowered them again. 'My friend.'

'I can hear in your voice that you think about her a lot,' I said. 'Tell me about her. You don't have to explain anything. Just talk to me about her. I'd like to know.'

There was a long moment's hesitation, but then a smile began creeping across Eloise's face. 'Olivia's beautiful. She has this dark brown hair. It's straight and shiny and comes down to here,' Eloise said, measuring against her upper arm. 'And most of the time she doesn't tie it back. She's got eyes that are so . . . They aren't brown but they aren't blue either. They're sort of a colour in between, like if you were looking into water. Into water in the river, where it's deep.' Eloise let out a blissful sigh.

'Okay, yes,' I said. 'She sounds very beautiful.'

'She's so clever. She's going to be a marine biologist, and she even has her own computer in her room. It's called her A-star computer, because she's going to get A-stars on her exams. Dad Powell bought it specially for her so she could study. Olivia wanted her own computer so that she didn't have to share with the boys, because they're always playing computer games. It's so hard to have a go, because they always pig it. But Dad Powell told Olivia it was too expensive for her to have her own. He says computers ought to be in the dining room so he knows we're not looking at porn or something. But Olivia told him she would get A-stars if she had a computer to study at. You have to get all A-stars on your exams to be a marine biologist.'

Eloise was becoming more animated. 'Olivia's got ocean pictures all over the walls of her room. I helped her get some of them. I look for them in magazines and cut them out for her. When I give them to her, she always puts them up on her wall with her other pictures.'

'That sounds very special,' I said when Eloise finally paused for breath. 'But I'm hearing you say "Dad Powell", so I'm thinking you're talking about Heddwen.'

'No,' she said matter-of-factly. There was a brief pause and then Eloise carried on as if I hadn't spoken. 'I've got her ring and I need to take it back to her, because I didn't steal it. You might hear someone say I stole it but I didn't.

'Do you want me to show it you? Because I've got it here.' Eloise pulled her handbag around and opened it. Lifting out a wodge of tissues, she pulled back the paper to reveal a small, delicate-looking ring with a silver setting in the shape of a pentagram. In the centre was a dark red stone. I could tell it was inexpensive, the kind of ring you'd find in a New Age gift shop along with the crystals and horoscopes.

'That's sardonyx,' Eloise said, touching the stone. 'It attracts good fortune. And friendship. That's why I have it, because Olivia is my best friend. She gave it to me.' Eloise slipped it on her finger. 'It fits me, see?

'I need to take the ring back. I didn't steal it. Olivia gave it to me. It's a gift from Olivia. But this other kid, Sam, he stole it from Olivia's bedroom and he blamed me. He said it was my fault. I'm just holding on to it to keep it safe. Sam's the one who stole it, not me. But I got it back from him and I need to show Olivia, so she doesn't worry about it. I want her to know it's safe.'

'Eloise . . .'

'I need you to help me make Mrs Thomas and Sue-Pugh understand that I didn't take it. I didn't steal it. I just have it to keep it safe and now I have to take it back. Olivia is expecting me. She's waiting for me, I promise. I didn't steal the ring. That's where everyone's confused. *I* didn't steal it. It's right here and I'm *trying* to get it back to Olivia. Don't you understand? *That's* my problem that you need to help me with.'

'I see.'

She looked over at me. We made eye contact, and I realized how little eye contact I'd had with her up to this point. Now, however, she pinned me down. 'Do you understand?' she asked. 'Do you *understand*?'

'Here,' I held out my hand towards the ring. 'If this needs to go back to Heddwen, I'm happy to take it for you. I'll explain you didn't steal it, that it was a misunderstanding.'

'*No*.' Clutching the ring against her body, Eloise looked anguished. 'You aren't listening to what I'm saying. *I* need to take it back.'

I withdrew my hand.

One hand over the other, pressing the ring in against her abdomen, she leaned away from me, her body growing rigid with anxiety.

A long pause stretched out between us, like a thin wire that I thought might snap at any moment, causing her to run.

'You know what?' I said in a quiet voice, 'I think we need a breather. I could do with a hot drink, couldn't you? It's cold in this room. What do you think?'

This sudden change of direction caught Eloise off guard. She looked at me blankly.

'Shall we go see what we can find? It wouldn't be a proper village hall if there wasn't a kitchen somewhere. And it wouldn't be a proper kitchen if it didn't have a kettle and some teabags, would it? Shall we go explore?'

Still stunned by the unexpectedness of my request, Eloise rose when I did and we went out into the hallway. The whole building was dim with winter dusk, so I switched on whatever lights I could find. The first room was large and empty except for a series of long folding tables that were collapsed and leaned against the far wall. The second room was small and completely empty. The third room was full of stacked plastic chairs. Then, at last, at the far end of the corridor, was a small kitchen. Sure enough, there was an electric kettle on the worktop. Picking it up, I peered in to see what shape it was in. Unlike much of Britain, our water was very, very soft, so while there was seldom a mineral build-up inside electric kettles there could be a gungy brownness, especially in ones that weren't used regularly. I rinsed it out, just to be sure, and then filled it and turned it on.

Eloise was going through the cupboards. 'Here're some teabags,' she said, and took down a large plastic tub.

Then disappointment, because when I opened the fridge there was no milk. Not that there was any reason to think someone would have left milk there, but we had been doing so well . . .

Eloise had already found two mugs and put teabags in when I showed her the empty fridge. 'We could just have it plain,' she said. 'I don't mind it that way, if it's not too strong. Maybe we could just use one bag between us.'

I could hear in her voice how much she wanted to do this, so I nodded.

Eloise took over from there, expertly popping the teabag in and out of both mugs without making it too strong. 'I could bring some milk next time,' she said.

'That's a good idea,' I said, smiling, because it meant she wanted there to be a next time.

We returned to our small room with the steaming mugs of tea and sat down at the table. I was reluctant to go back to the topic of Heddwen/Olivia because it had clearly been so distressing for Eloise, but equally because it had been so confusing to me. I wanted an opportunity to check things out with Sue-Pugh to give myself a more objective perspective on what had been going on at the Powells'. I was also reluctant to venture into any other conversational topics that Eloise might consider confrontational, as she had become so withdrawn and self-conscious on other occasions. This late in our time together, the best tack seemed to be distraction.

'I wonder if you could help me with something,' I said, and lifted up my brown satchel. Everything I used with the various groups of different children lived in this satchel. It was a bit of a Tardis, looking quite ordinary on the outside but full of marvels within, and so I opened it and peered inside. I had no plan for what to do if we weren't going to talk.

Pulling out a folder full of materials I used with one of the enrichment groups, I lay it open on the table. 'See this set of cards? They have feeling words written on them and they are meant to be matched up with this set of photographs, but the kids mess them up when playing with them. So every time I put them away, they are all mixed up. I'm going to see these children next after our session is over, so I'm wondering if you could help me sort these out.'

Eloise brightened. 'I can do that easily. Here. Give me them.'

She spread the photos out. Picking up the cards, she shuffled through them, seeing what was written on them. Then she started laying them on the pictures that should accompany them. Most were straightforward – happy, excited, angry – but a few were more subtle – trapped, safe, jealous – and these required careful consideration of the photographs.

Eloise was chattering now, asking me if anything else needed organizing. She pulled the satchel closer and peered in, then expressed exaggerated shock at the state of it. 'You could have a lot more room in this,' she said. 'You should let me organize it for you. Can I turn it out?' And before I said yay or nay on the matter, the contents of my satchel were dumped unceremoniously on the tabletop.

'We only have ten minutes left,' I said dubiously.

'Not to worry,' she replied brightly, and set about putting my pens and markers into order.

Nursing my mug of tea, I watched her. The anxiety Eloise had shown earlier had been dispelled entirely. She was enjoying this, just as she had enjoyed making the tea. Competence radiated from her, but also an open willingness to be helpful, to do a good job.

I pondered the situation with Heddwen. Why had she been renamed 'Olivia'? What purpose did that serve? And what about this ring? I assumed it was Heddwen's. Had Eloise stolen it? There was a magical-thinking aspect to Eloise's version of what was going on, the ring symbolizing a friendship that didn't exist. Was it anxiety about this that made her completely incapable of speaking about it?

Thinking through all this, I felt a twinge of sadness. What would work well here was old-fashioned talk therapy. My sense was of a lonely girl, adrift, who desperately needed sincere, focused attention. Not for the first time, I wished we had the resources to provide such services, even as I knew it was completely impossible. In our large, rural county, children had a difficult time accessing treatment for mental health issues. Most services were clustered in the large cities, the nearest of which for us was over the border in England, a three-hour drive away. With an issue requiring that much travel, you could go for a consultation, but ongoing treatment was unrealistic. The services we had locally were stretched woefully thin. Even money couldn't solve that problem. Parents who wanted private treatment for their children still had to face a long wait or travel unreasonably long distances.

Foster children and other children in the system struggled to receive any treatment at all. Ben Stone, the child psychologist working for Social Services, had more than two thousand clients on his list, so while he endeavoured to see all the children at one point or another, his role was largely confined to testing and consultation. Most of the resources for mental health went on supporting adoptive families. So many foster children who came up for adoption had such dysfunctional backgrounds that the transition to a new family was often difficult, even when they were going into loving, welcoming homes. Providing therapy at this point increased the chances that the adoption would be successful, and the child would not be returned to state care, so this was where the resources went, but it left very little money for mental health treatment of children still in the system. Charities like mine stepped in at this point, and counsellors like me became part of the helping landscape. In my current position, I was able to offer Eloise six cognitive behavioural therapy-based sessions.

I'd just wasted one of them.

chapter five

Cognitive behavioural therapy (CBT) is a psychotherapy treatment that takes a pragmatic approach to psychological problems, breaking them down into five areas: situations, thoughts, emotions, physical sensations or feelings, and actions. The idea is that these are all part of the whole, are all interconnected with each other, and hence what we think about situations influences our emotions and ultimately what we do. For example, the situation where you are in an overcrowded room may produce the thought: 'How will I get out?' Thinking this then produces an emotion such as fear, and the fear turns to the physical feeling of panic. You react by running out of the room. The goal in CBT is to help the sufferer develop awareness of this pattern of events, and eventually help them learn how to challenge and change the problematic thoughts before they stimulate feelings and actions.

I was trained in this therapeutic intervention because it was useful 'in the field', meaning that it could be done in almost any setting and did not require a special environment or a long investment of time. This was the programme my charity felt was most appropriate for Eloise. However, I was having a hard time getting my head around how to focus on Eloise's particular problem – her obsession with Heddwen – within the format I had. Stalking was not something I had had previous experience of as a therapist. My five or six sessions of CBT felt like puny weaponry with which to attack this, especially as so far I hadn't even managed to get Eloise to acknowledge this was the problem.

The next Thursday afternoon Eloise was waiting eagerly for me outside the village hall. When she saw my car pull up, she smiled broadly and came running over.

'Look!' she said, her voice ebullient. 'I brought milk!' She pulled a pint bottle from her jacket pocket. 'It's semi-skimmed. I hope that's okay. Do you like semi-skimmed? Or would you rather have had whole milk? My foster mum says tea tastes terrible with whole milk in it, but I quite like it.'

'Semi-skimmed's good,' I said.

'Shall we make tea first? We can make it and take it with us to the room. That'll warm us up, because it's perishing today, isn't it? That room is going to be baltic. Shall we do that? I thought to bring teabags as well, because those in the kitchen might be really old, but I didn't, because I didn't know if you wanted me to. I should have, now that I think about it. I can next week. Shall we make the tea first?'

I had never seen Eloise anywhere near this animated and it surprised me, both for the degree of enthusiasm she was showing for a cup of tea and for the contrast to what had been, for me, her previous norm.

Inside the village hall, I turned lights on and put my satchel in our room, before going down to the kitchen where Eloise already had the kettle boiling.

'I appreciate your bringing us some milk,' I said. 'And thank you for making the tea.'

'I like to make tea,' she replied with a smile.

As we were walking back to the room, Eloise said, 'I thought maybe I could sort out the rest of your satchel for you. Last time I did the pens and things, but they probably didn't stay sorted, so I've brought along some little sandwich bags, the kind you can press together at the top. And I'll put all the cards in order this time. You had a lot of stuff at the bottom that was all mixed up.'

'Yes, you were very helpful last time, but I think we need to work on other things first. We'll leave ten minutes at the end for cleaning the satchel.'

My saying that was as if I had pushed down a shutter. Eloise literally closed up. There was a tightening of her jaw muscles, a puckering of the skin at the edges of her eyes and then a sharp intake of breath. It was as if she didn't breathe after that. Eloise put her tea on the tabletop. She didn't touch it again.

'I know in your heart you really want help getting your problems sorted out,' I said softly, 'because you've come to me twice to ask for help. I know you're serious about this. But whenever we start to talk about what's bothering you, it seems like you feel too frightened to go forward.'

Staring down at her hands, Eloise lifted her shoulders in a faint shrug. 'I just wanted to do your bag,' she said in a tiny voice.

'Yes, and that is very, very kind of you. We'll make special time for that, because I appreciate so much that you want to help me, but let's talk a little bit about the scary feelings first. I would like to understand more about them, about what parts feel frightening to you.'

Eloise lowered her head to where her chin was almost against her school tie.

'It's completely normal to feel scared when you are trying to change things. I have lots of experience working with kids and I know how frightening they find it. It's all right to have those feelings. It's all right for you to be just as you are, feeling just what you feel. You don't need to be different. You don't need to be stronger. You don't need to be more in control. You're okay just as you are.'

Eloise kept her head down.

'What do you feel will happen if we talk about your problems?' I asked.

A faint shrug.

Silence lingered. Sitting back in a relaxed manner on my chair, I tried to exude tranquillity, hoping the anxiety would ease for Eloise if she could sense that I was not made anxious by her behaviour. I hoped she would find courage in not being pressured to speak.

I sipped my tea. Hers grew cold. I felt bad about this. She had been so happy about bringing the milk and making the tea for me that I wished I hadn't ruined it by trying to get on with the job.

'Here's what I see,' I said at last. 'This thing with Heddwen . . . it must feel awful to want to be with somebody so much, to ache for their attention, but then they don't want you around. You can't stop feeling the way you feel, but that's what everyone wants you to do. That must be hard to contend with. And it must be confusing, because here you are on one side and the whole rest of the world seems to be on the other side, fighting you, and they don't understand how much it hurts you.'

Eloise pulled her lower lip in between her teeth to keep her chin from trembling.

'I'm sorry this hurts so much,' I said.

A tear ran down her cheek. She lifted one hand and wiped it away but then a second came close behind it.

I'd hoped that, in articulating the problem, Eloise would feel a sense of being understood, and while I knew it was likely to make her cry, I hoped it would be with relief. However, this didn't happen. As Eloise began to cry I felt tension in the room increase, not decrease, and this made me wary that she was going to run. She wasn't agreeing with what I was saying, as I had hoped she would. She just sat rigidly, trying to keep the tears in check, and for the most part she was succeeding. I didn't want to push things, so I said no more.

Silence.

My mind was hyper alert, trying to read what was happening, trying to discern the best course. Should I reiterate my sympathy? Should I continue trying to put into words what I sensed she was feeling? Would this eventually bring her relief? Or would it push her into fleeing or self-harm or worse? Should I just shut up and let the silence be?

Eloise kept her head down. She was no longer crying. The tears had never developed past the two or three that had trickled down her cheek.

For lack of something better to say, I reached over and moved her mug towards her and said, 'Your tea will be cold soon.'

Eloise looked up and then to the mug. She reached out for it and took a sip.

Again, the silence.

Then she said in a quiet voice, 'I brought some sandwich bags for your pens.' There was a slight accusatory tone, almost petulant, as if I'd purposely spoiled things.

'That was kind of you. You were being thoughtful about how you could keep me organized.'

For the first time since we'd sat down, she looked me in the eye. 'Can I do it?'

'Yes, go ahead.'

Wiping her eyes with the heel of her hand, Eloise stood up and got my satchel. She opened it and began pulling items out and setting them in front of her. 'This is, like, a seriously weird table,' she said, her tone casual, as if all that had gone before had not happened. 'It's not got much tabletop, but it's got such long legs. Kind of useless, really.' There was a pause, then she added, 'Like me.'

My instinct, of course, was to rebut her statement, to say no, of course she wasn't useless. The irony was that at that very moment she was literally being the opposite of useless by sorting out the contents of my bag. I didn't say that, however, thinking perhaps it would be more helpful to accept that these were her legitimate feelings instead of telling her she was wrong to feel this way.

Noticing my silence, she raised her eyes to me, so I nodded. 'Yes, I think it's a weird little table too, but I rather like it. I wonder what it was made for.'

'Maybe you're supposed to have really tall chairs.'

'Yes, maybe.'

And so it went on, innocent, fairly meaningless chat back and forth as she cleaned out my satchel, matching up all the pens by brand and sorting them into sandwich bags before putting them back in. She then stacked the various therapy cards in their corresponding groups.

I watched her as she worked. Were we wasting the session? Back in the old days when play therapy was a common treatment for mental health problems, this would have been considered appropriate. These days, however, I was expected to move on to a new child after six sessions. It would take a fair amount of haggling with my charity to arrange for more time, especially if there was no evidence I was following a prescribed format. We were in an age of accountability. I had to file a report on each meeting I held with a child, charting our progress over the six sessions. What was I going to say here? 'Let child clean out my work materials'?

'Can you tell me about the first time you met Heddwen?' I asked.

Eloise stopped dead. She had been putting a pair of small hand puppets back into my bag; her fingers froze over the opening to the satchel.

'Had you just arrived? What do you recall about going to the Powells'?'

Gradually Eloise came back to life. Lowering her hand, she lay the puppets on the table beside the satchel. Taking a deep breath and exhaling audibly, she sat down in her chair. She didn't look at me. Her attention appeared to go to her mug, and she pulled it over.

'My things were in a bin bag,' she said quietly. 'My *nain* said I could have a suitcase, but it was too big. The social worker who came to take me away said I couldn't have one that big. That was okay because it was ugly. It was, like, a million years old and had scuffs all over it. It looked like something she'd found at the tip, so I didn't want it anyway. The social worker gave me a bin bag to put my things in and said to hurry up, because we were late. It was a long drive from my *nain*'s, so the social worker said I couldn't take so much time.'

Eloise paused and sipped from the mug. She peered into it afterwards, as if she hadn't expected what was in there. Then she drained it.

'That's the day you went to the Powells'?' I asked.

She nodded. 'I didn't get there until evening, and when I went inside it smelled funny. They were having scouse for tea and I hate scouse. When *Nain* made it, she knew I didn't like it, so I didn't have to eat it. I could have bread and butter instead, but I was scared because maybe they wouldn't know that.'

'You were worried about having to eat food you didn't like?'

Eloise nodded. 'And then I was to take my stuff upstairs because that's where my room was going to be, but when I got about halfway up, the bin bag broke. I had my CDs at the bottom of it and the corner of one cut through the bag, and all my stuff fell down the stairs. This boy laughed at me. I don't remember his name now because he was one of the other foster kids, and he went away soon after. Aled or Alan or something. I don't remember. But he was, like, fifteen, and he laughed, and I thought I was going to cry because it was a big mess and I was embarrassed, but I didn't want them to see. I didn't want them to think straightaway that I was a baby.'

'Having your belongings fall out on the stairs would be upsetting, even if no one laughed at you. What happened next?'

'Olivia got up from the table. She came over and helped me pick up my things. Then she carried them upstairs with me and showed me where my room was.'

'Heddwen?'

Eloise didn't look at me. 'I said to her, "You're having scouse, aren't you? I hate scouse and I don't think I can eat it, but I'm very hungry."

'Olivia said, "What kind of things do you like?" I said I liked sausages and chips and pizza, and some things that have gravy on them, like steak pie, and I liked fish pie that my *nain* made because it didn't have smoked fish in it. So the truth is I like lots of things. I just don't like scouse. I said that on scouse night at my *nain*'s, she let me have bread and butter instead.'

Eloise paused. 'I was afraid she was going to tell me I had to eat the scouse anyway, because that's what my mum used to do. Mum said, in her day, children ate what they were served and I would too, so she used to make me sit at the table until the food was all gone. She didn't care if it made me sick. It did once. I did a little upchuck right at the table and my mum hit me with a coat hanger. I had marks all up and down my arms.'

'Scouse has given you a rough time, hasn't it?'

Eloise nodded. 'But Olivia said her family wouldn't make me eat it. She said, "Come in my room. I've got some chocolate. I'll give you some." So I went in her room and she had one of those Terry's oranges and it was new. It was still whole. And she opened it and she gave me *four* pieces. Just for me.'

'How kind of her. She understood how worried and upset you were, didn't she?'

Eloise smiled, and for the first time, she lifted her head and looked at me. 'Yes. I was feeling awful about my *nain* not wanting me any more, but Olivia made me glad I'd gone there.'

'This helps me understand how important Heddwen was to you.'

'Please don't call her Heddwen,' Eloise said softly, her head down. 'That's such an ugly name. Heth – th – th – the. It sounds like you're going to say "Heather" but you don't. It's like you're going to ask Heather when? And it's even uglier written down. Like Head-win. Edwin. Like a boy's name.'

'How does she feel about being called Olivia?' I asked.

Eloise shrugged. An uncomfortable moment followed, as if my question had been a chastisement, but then her features softened again. 'I called her Olivia on that first night. She smiled at me, but said that wasn't her name. I asked if she minded if I called her that anyway, because it was my favourite name and she was so beautiful. It made her special. She liked that. She said how sweet I was. She liked that I thought she was special.'

chapter six

Christmas came and went. I had three weeks off from my work with the charity and didn't return until the first week in January.

During this period of endless Christmas parties, I ran into Meleri on a couple of occasions. She was the social worker for the other foster children who were still at the Powells', and she told me that, much to everyone's relief, Eloise had not shown up. Checking in with Sue-Pugh in early January before I went back to work confirmed that Eloise had also not run away at any point over Christmas. I suspect this was mostly due to the weather, as we'd had a succession of snowstorms during the holiday period which had been disruptive to everyone, but it was reassuring to know that Eloise was behaving herself.

When the second Thursday in January rolled around, there in the village hall car park was Eloise, waiting for me in the dim light of a midwinter's afternoon, milk and teabags clutched tightly in a carrier bag. She greeted me fulsomely.

Eloise made tea for us. Pride in her competence at this task shone through. The milk was fresh; the teabags were from a brand-new packet that she had bought with her own money. She even had one of the ubiquitous sandwich bags to place over the opened packet of tea so that it would stay fresh for next time. 'Should we leave it there in the kitchen?' she asked me. 'Do other people come in?' A few moments passed in deliberation over whether we minded if they used our teabags or not. Eloise decided she would take the teabags with her and bring them again next Thursday. Then we went down to the room.

For the most part I'm all in favour of CBT because it encourages us to become aware of our thoughts. Too many of us go through life without bothering to notice what we're thinking or to pay attention to unhelpful cycles of thought that make us feel anxious or get us into trouble. CBT's pragmatic structure means that it can successfully deliver help in a fairly short space of time. It does require commitment from the participant, which is sometimes hard to muster, and the approach isn't for everyone, but on the whole I found it a useful tool, and its short, targeted approach makes it invaluable for cash- and time-strapped services that otherwise could provide no therapeutic intervention at all.

The biggest drawback of our charity's programme was that we were limited to providing six CBT sessions per client. This was due to both a cost issue and a manpower one. There just weren't enough trained professionals to go around, especially in the volunteer sector which served the most vulnerable. When I had been brought in to work with Eloise, the assumption from my charity was that I would take her through the six-session CBT course. I was beginning to feel pressured because of this. Eloise had complex issues and a complicated past. I had no doubt CBT would be helpful to her if I could get her to commit to it, but so far I had not managed even the first stage of the structured programme and this was already our third session. I knew I could probably extend our time together if I could engage her, but I had to start making these sessions worthwhile.

Once we were seated at the table, I took out a notebook and pen. 'While we're drinking our tea, we're going to try something,' I said. 'I want you to relax a moment . . .'

Eloise was anything but relaxed. The minute she saw the notebook she tensed, and by the time I'd finished speaking her head was down, her arms wrapped around her body.

'Nothing's going to happen. All I want us to do is sit quietly and let our bodies relax. Just notice your muscles. Your shoulder muscles, the back of your neck. Let them relax.'

This wasn't fooling Eloise. She knew I was up to something.

'There are no tricks here, Eloise. This is a relaxation exercise, nothing more. All we're going to do is sit quietly. We're going to let our bodies relax and then gently notice the thoughts that are going through our heads. Nothing more. Absolutely nothing more. Just notice the thoughts. Not do anything with them. Not worry about what they are. Not try to make them stop or change them to different thoughts or anything at all. Just notice what's there. For a minute, okay? That's all. Sixty seconds and then we'll stop.' I took my watch off and lay it flat on the table. 'Let's try that.'

The minute passed.

Eloise had not moved, neither before nor now. She sat, as if spell struck.

'Here's what I noticed going through my head while we were sitting,' I said. 'At first I had thoughts about being here, doing this. I was very conscious of trying to notice my thoughts. Then I sort of forgot about doing that and just had thoughts. I thought about how cold the room is. That made me think about the weather. I wondered if there was going to be a storm. Then the minute was up. These are "thought trains", these different topics. We call them this because once we start thinking about a topic, there are usually several related thoughts about it. One of my thought trains was about the temperature. I thought about being cold, which made me think about it getting colder, which made me think about the winter weather. Those were all related thoughts. How about you? What did you notice you were thinking about in that minute?'

Eloise said nothing.

'What was the first thought you noticed?'

She was totally blanking me.

'Sometimes it takes a bit of practice to learn how to do this. Most of the time, we're inside our thoughts. We don't actually notice when they go from one thing to another, because we are riding the train, not looking at it. Let's try it again. See if you can notice the different things you think about during the minute.'

I checked my watch again and we sat through another minute. During this time, all my thoughts were pretty much on whether or not Eloise was going to cooperate.

Nothing happened. Eloise continued sitting there, letting her tea go cold. She wouldn't speak.

'I see your muscles tensing and this makes me think you are finding this a challenge. Is that so?'

No response.

'It would be helpful for me to know what's happening for you when we do this. Can you tell me how you're feeling?'

No response.

'Shall I explain why we're doing this? It's because our minds create thoughts. Millions of thoughts. All the time. This is entirely normal. It's what minds do, what minds are for. And among these millions of thoughts are different kinds. Some are constructive thoughts that help us do things that we want to do. You thought about getting milk so that we can have a cuppa. That was a constructive thought. Some thoughts are just for fun. I saw a video of a dancing cat this morning, and every time I think about it, it makes me laugh. Thinking about that dancing cat is a fun thought. Other thoughts are unsettling. When my daughter and I were out last weekend, we got trapped in a public garden by a big, barky dog. When I think about the dog, I worry about going back to that place, because I might encounter him again, so the dog thought unsettles me. And some thoughts are just plain destructive. They make us feel bad without helping us find a solution. For instance, if I make a mistake, sometimes I hear a voice in my head say, "You're stupid. You'll never do that right." That isn't true. I do lots of things right. So that thought is just being mean to me for no good reason. It's a destructive thought.'

Eloise sat, head down, arms around herself.

'It's quite useful to learn how to recognize these different thoughts . . .'

Eloise didn't look up.

The session had a depressing aura. All I could hear was my own voice. Everything I said sounded boring and unengaging. We had started so cheerfully with the enthusiastic tea-making only to end up sitting in this dank little room at this bizarre table, the tea growing cold, silence and anxiety our only company.

I pulled the satchel over. 'Shall we play a game of cards?'

Eloise still didn't respond.

I took a deck out. 'Do you know how to play Snap?'

She gave a faint shake of her head. My spirits rose at this feeble sign of life.

'It's fun. I'll explain.' I shuffled the deck.

'Can I go to the toilet first?'

'Yes, of course.'

I shuffled the cards several times as I waited for her to return. It felt good to be active again after the long frozen silence. I noticed how tense my own posture had become and rotated my shoulders to loosen muscles.

It didn't take as long this time for me to realize she wasn't coming back. After five or six minutes, a sinking sensation – starting first in my throat and then sliding into my chest – accompanied my growing awareness, as did a few of those destructive thoughts, mostly about how stupid I was to let myself be fooled again.

I went out into the hallway. It was empty. No one. The light was off in the kitchen. The light was off in the toilet. Everywhere was silent and still. She'd disappeared.

And she disappeared properly. Eloise didn't return home to her foster family in the village that afternoon. She was gone for eight days, meaning she missed our next session as well. When she was finally found, it was in the Powells' garage.

I felt frustrated and confused. Eloise wanted help, but then, no, she didn't want help. She was cooperative, but then, no, she wasn't cooperative. She understood the problem of stalking Heddwen, but then, no, that wasn't the problem. And there were so many constraints on our situation, ranging from the unpleasant little white room, to the structured CBT course that took no prisoners, to the ridiculous set-up that left an impulsive, suicidal teenager way too free to come and go as she wanted.

Meleri was no longer Eloise's supervising social worker, but I could think of no one else who would better understand my need to vent on this case, so we met for lunch in a small fish-and-chips restaurant down on the seafront.

It was a bitterly cold day of sharp, sleety showers. This was well before the tourist season, so there was none of the usual jostling for seats on the long cafeteria-style tables. In fact, on that particular day, it was only Meleri and me, along with the occasional customer who came in for a takeaway.

As Sue-Pugh was now Eloise's caseworker, Meleri wasn't up to date on what was going on, but that was all right. I wasn't looking for a consultation. I wasn't even looking for solutions, because at that point I wasn't sure there were any. I just needed sympathy and a listening ear, and Meleri was good at both of those.

What could I do with this girl? I asked. She continued to stalk Heddwen, and I didn't know how to get her to even acknowledge that there was a problem with that, much less stop it. She continued to run away at the slightest upset, and I didn't know from one week to the next whether she would even turn up to the session. She wanted help, but everything I did seemed to frighten her into paralytic silence.

We were sitting across from one another at the far end of one of the long tables. We both had fish and chips served in paper-lined red plastic baskets. Meleri also had mushy peas, dumped unceremoniously over her chips. She slid her arm down the smooth, white Formica tabletop to grab the vinegar. A few moments' silence passed as we adjusted our seasonings and picked through the food, looking for bits cool enough to eat. Then Meleri began talking about Eloise's diagnosis of depression and anxiety. This was the only official diagnosis Eloise had, a label she'd acquired at thirteen. 'I saw this, and I'm like, no shit, Sherlock,' Meleri said. 'One sibling dead because of abuse, one sibling removed from the home because of abuse, she'd been prostituted by nine and rejected by what family she had left at thirteen. I'd be more concerned if she wasn't depressed. So, yes, I'm not too surprised that she's unwilling to chance looking any of this in the face.'

While it wasn't much to cling to, I was heartened by the fact that Eloise carried the diagnosis of anxiety and depression and not an attachment disorder or one of the more serious attention disorders. I asked Meleri what she knew of Eloise's treatment. She said that antidepressants had been considered, but because of her young age the decision was made not to offer them. The concern revolved around Eloise's suicidal behaviour. While she had threatened on several occasions, she had not yet followed through with an attempt. The concern was that the antidepressants could make this suicidal behaviour worse, but also that the tablets themselves could be a source of poisoning, if she decided to tongue them and save them up.

There was a thinking pause, and Meleri reached for the vinegar again, and then she said, 'I wonder how much of Eloise's behaviour with you is self-sabotage. As in "I want the help offered, but I know I'm not going to manage what you want, so I'll wreck it before I start."'

This had crossed my mind, so I nodded.

'That,' she said, 'or possibly it's about rejection. "I want help, but I know you're going to reject me at some point, so I'll do the rejecting first."'

I considered this.

'Perhaps Eloise is acting out her feelings,' Meleri said, 'rather the way younger children do with play, where they continually repeat a theme. I remember one little girl who had been badly neglected and very often left with nothing to eat. When she was in foster care she repeatedly pretended to make you food. She'd offer it to you, but if you tried to accept it, she'd snatch it away. She'd always laugh and we thought it was a game at first, but then we began to realize she was taking back the food from us just as food had always been snatched away from her, and that was the important part of processing her abuse, the taking away. Could Eloise be doing something similar? Processing, say, her own past experiences of asking for help but not receiving it? Each time she asks for help, you offer it then she rejects it. Over and over. Maybe it's code for "Here's what it feels like to be me. Experience what it is like to want others to engage with you but always be rebuffed."'

My mind didn't think in those kinds of parallels, which was one of the reasons I found conversations with Meleri energizing. I naturally shied away from interpreting others' behaviour in ways I couldn't objectively verify, because I was chary of the fact everything was filtered through my own worldview. I nonetheless found that Meleri's interpretive thinking enriched my own understanding, even when I disagreed with it. Inevitably, it broadened the scope of my own observations.

All that was left of our lunch were the tasty little crumbs of batter and crispy ends of chips in the bottom of our red latticework baskets. Meleri paused a moment to pick through them.

'So, there I am,' I said in summary, 'she asks for help. I offer help. She clams up. She comes to the CBT sessions. I offer the CBT work. She clams up. I have no idea where to go from here, because the only time she engages with me is when we make tea. The moment I say, "What's the problem?", the conversation is over.'

'The answer seems straightforward to me,' Meleri said, looking up. She smiled. 'You need to make tea.'

chapter seven

As is so often the case with an offhand remark, there was truth at the heart of it. Eloise and I did connect during those first ten minutes of the session when she made tea for us. After that point she became more withdrawn and anxious.

I tried deconstructing the meetings; trying to understand what worked for Eloise about the tea and again at the end of each session when tidying up my satchel. Was it because she was in control? Or because she felt useful and valued? Or were they simply displacement activities that helped her avoid focusing on the more painful issues I was there to help her with? None of the above? All of the above?

'Make tea.' How could I get therapeutic mileage out of that? How could making tea translate into a means for stopping her stalking Heddwen Powell? I didn't have a clue. All I did know was that my six CBT sessions were unlikely to be the answer, so I needed to change tactics.

My first port of call was my charity to talk over my options.

Our local director was a woman named Lynn Davis. She was older, perhaps in her late fifties, tall, slim, and always immaculately groomed in a casual way that I had not originally recognized as a clue to her class. When I'd first come to the UK, the whole British class thing was a complete mystery to me. My ear was not trained to discern the accents which immediately gave natives valuable information about the speaker's background and social status. I did not know the many words that were subtle indicators of class, such as 'toilet', 'lavatory', 'WC' and 'loo', as there were no such differentiations in the US. I didn't recognize which first names went with which classes, which nicknames, or how you addressed a lady versus a Lady. I was much better at it now, but Lynn had been an object lesson in how wary I needed to be.

When I first started working for the charity, she'd been my instructor. Much of our intake training revolved around learning to be non-judgemental, a skill I'd always felt confident about. Until I met Lynn. She could sniff out expectations faster than a rat after rubbish. She caught me out on my very first morning and it wasn't even in the training session but while we were having a coffee. Earlier in the day Lynn had mentioned the village where she lived. I remembered that the village primary school there had recently built an award-winning playground. Knowing she had young children and wanting to make pleasant conversation, I asked how her children were enjoying it. 'You're making an *assumption*,' she'd replied sharply. 'I tell you where I live, and you assume my children go to the local school. Rule One: Never make an assumption.'

She was right, of course. I had assumed. I felt embarrassed to be called out on it, as we'd just completed an hour's training on not being judgemental, but also because it had been such an innocent remark. As it turned out, her children were at boarding school two hundred miles away, something I might have picked up on had I been better at reading accents, but there I was, stuck only with my basic knowledge, caught out making an assumption after a forty-five minute lecture on not doing so.

The encounter had left me leery of Lynn. That had literally been my first day of training, and her correction established her firmly in my mind as a no-nonsense, no-holds-barred type of person. This proved to be an accurate assessment. Lynn said what she thought and let the chips fall where they may. She was, however, also very good at her job. Her understanding of the broader needs of the children the charity served and her ability to provide thoroughly trained volunteers was impeccable, so it was normally worth the ego bruising to learn from her.

Even now, however, I didn't feel entirely at ease in her company, so I didn't go in to see Lynn more often than necessary. I had an annual review, but beyond that I generally tried to get on with things, turn my written reports in on time and not call undue attention to myself. On this occasion, however, there seemed to be no other alternative. I'd been sent out to do a specific job and that wasn't working. I needed more flexibility.

This occasion wasn't much different from my other meetings with Lynn. The first thing she did was make me go carefully step by step through the CBT programme I was using to ensure I knew thoroughly what I was teaching and how to carry it out correctly. It was a perfectly reasonable thing for her to check on; however, I immediately felt guilty of something in the way you do when you see a policeman. I felt certain she'd find I was doing the CBT script wrong in some way and the failure with Eloise would turn out to be my fault.

When I'd talked my way through the complete programme, Lynn took me back to the beginning of it. Have you done the introduction? she asked. Yes, but there was no response. Have you completed Stage 1? No, because I wasn't able to complete the introduction. No, I can't get a response. No. No.

Lynn sat back in her desk chair and gave me a long, appraising look. 'You haven't got very far then, have you?'

'No.' And I felt about six inches high.

Lynn smiled pleasantly. 'I can see you're right. We'll have to do something differently.'

Eloise was waiting outside the village hall when I arrived the next Thursday afternoon. She was clutching the teabags, but when I got out of the car she didn't come over.

'I didn't know if you'd want to see me,' she said, her voice reticent.

'Yes, of course I do. I missed you last week.'

We stopped in the kitchen first to make the tea, but Eloise remained subdued. I let her do it all, hoping this would break the ice, and she did but without saying much of anything. We took our mugs down to the room in silence.

'I've had time to do some thinking,' I said. 'And I've decided we need a different approach.'

As I spoke, I could see the expression on Eloise's face changing. She was already more subdued than usual, but there was a literal closing down taking place, almost as if blinds were being pulled down behind her eyes.

'Hold on,' I said. 'Hear me out. You've got choices here.'

Eloise regarded me. 'You're going to tell me we're stopping, aren't you? You're done helping me. That's okay. I don't care.'

'No, that wasn't what I was going to say.'

'I don't care. I really don't.'

'*Eloise*.'

She shrugged.

'Okay, stop. Stop it. Listen. Do you know what I'm hearing?' I said. 'Right this minute, I'm hearing that you want to cut your losses. You think I'm going to say that I want to stop, so you're going to stop first.'

'Nooo.'

A moment's impasse. I was half expecting her to say she was going to go to the toilet or in some other way manage to walk out. We were teetering on that spot.

'What I was *going* to say was that when one approach doesn't work out, I don't just give up. I try something else. *That's* what I was trying to say.'

Eloise kept her head down.

'You do such a good job of helping – making our drinks, organizing my satchel – that I was thinking maybe you'd like to help me do something else.'

While she didn't go so far as to make eye contact, she tipped her head.

'On Wednesdays, I go to Pen-y-Garth to run an enrichment

group. I wondered if, instead of doing this each week, you would like to come along and help me there.'

'Help you do what?' she asked.

'Be my assistant. They're all little kids. The oldest is only seven. They all have problems that make it hard to learn, so they need quite a lot of one-to-one attention. I thought maybe you would like to give me a hand with them. Instead of coming here on Thursdays.'

Her brow crinkled in puzzlement.

'Does that sound like something you might enjoy?' I asked.

'I don't know,' she said uncertainly. 'I don't know much about little children.'

'Remember that very first day when you came to the office building in Harewood? Remember sitting in the circle with the children there while they played a game? They were trying to guess the labels on their foreheads. Remember that? This group is much the same. The children will be playing games or doing activities, and you can help me keep things organized. That's why my satchel was such a mess. I'm so busy I just throw things back in. You could help me stay tidy.'

Her face was brightening.

'Would you like that?' I asked.

She nodded slowly. 'I guess so.'

Lynn and I had decided to include Eloise in the enrichment group as a means of building a rapport that would eventually allow me to carry out a more traditional treatment approach. It also subtly tackled the stalking issue. Eloise had been most prone to going over to the Powells' on Wednesday afternoons, as both the Powell parents worked until 6 p.m., so Heddwen was home alone with the two foster children. If I picked Eloise up from school and we went to Pen-y-Garth, it would be almost 6 p.m. by the time I got her home.

As we drove out the next Wednesday, I told Eloise about the children in the group. There were eight, aged between five and seven. All came from deprived homes. One had Down's syndrome, one was autistic, one was dyspraxic and the five others had non-specific developmental delays that were interfering with their progress at school. I explained briefly what to expect, who would need help with the toilet, who would be very gregarious, who would run and hide. Pen-y-Garth was an inland area, so I also mentioned that most of the children were first-language Welsh and a couple were not quite bilingual, which meant we usually had a hash of English and Welsh going on, because I too was not quite bilingual.

Eloise looked over in alarm. 'I don't speak Welsh.'

'You'll be all right. Everyone is patient with one another.'

She took a deep breath and looked out the window. 'I failed my Welsh class. Twice.'

'It doesn't matter.'

A long pause followed, and then Eloise said, 'My *nain* would only speak Welsh.'

'Did you find that hard?'

She nodded. 'She said that's how I'd learn, but I couldn't get it. That's why I had to come back here.'

'I suspect your returning had more to do with your dad,' I

replied. 'I understand he went back to prison quite soon after you moved in with your grandmother and him.'

'Yes, but if I could have learned Welsh, my *nain* might have kept me.'

'It's so easy to feel like things are your fault when they go wrong, but that's not what happened here. It wasn't about Welsh. You were moved because your dad went to prison and your *nain* was just too old to take care of someone your age.'

We rode a few miles in silence.

'My mum thought Welsh people were stupid. She said, who would want to learn a language that hardly anybody speaks? She said if it was French or something, that would make sense because you could go on holiday and speak to the French people. But learning Welsh is a waste because you can't use it anywhere.'

'Except this is Wales and that's their language, and you can use it right here, because a lot of people, like your dad and your grandma, do speak it,' I said.

'Yes, but she still said it's stupid, because everyone here speaks English as well. Pretty soon everyone in the world will speak English, so that's the most useful language.'

'I think the idea is that Welsh people have the right to speak their own language in their own country. It doesn't matter who speaks it elsewhere,' I replied.

'My mum would really lose her shit over it,' Eloise replied. 'Like this once, she tore the pages out of my books when she saw they were in Welsh. She tore up my homework once and stuffed it in my mouth because I was speaking Welsh to her. She said I was giving her cheek.'

'She did have strong feelings, didn't she? I'm sorry that happened.'

'I didn't know I had a Welsh grandmother then. *Mamgu*. That's the word for it in Welsh. Or *nain*. She likes *Nain* better. And she didn't want me to speak English. She kept telling me not to be a dirty *Saes*.'

'That must have been confusing for you,' I said, 'if one side told you Welsh was bad and wanted you to speak English, and the other side told you English was bad and wanted you to speak Welsh.'

Eloise shrugged. 'I was used to it. My mum and dad hated everything about each other. Including me.'

chapter eight

'Miss! Miss! See? My *gath wedi* scratch me!' This was Ffion, dancing around me even before I had the door shut. A tall, slim six-year-old with a tangled cloud of ashy-blonde hair framing her face, Ffion had an incredible line in fractured English. She was trying to tell me that her cat had scratched her arm and was very excited to show the injury. '*Edrychwch! Edrychwch!*' she said again and again, lifting her arm up first to me and then to Eloise. Eloise flinched back as if Ffion were the one about to scratch.

I introduced the other children as they came running up – Lewis, Bethan, Bryn, Jack, Katie, Rhian and Buddug – and moved us on into the room to get everyone to sit in a circle on the big rug.

We were in the old village school, built in 1879. There was a new school at the other end of the village, which left this one free for community activities. It had only two rooms, both of which were cavernous and quite chilly. The toilets were outside in a small stone shed behind the building. Originally heated by open fires, each of the rooms now had storage heaters which were safer but inadequate for their purpose, especially by late afternoon when they'd released most of their stored-up heat. Despite being chilly, however, it was a wonderful location because it was so generously proportioned and well built; and best of all, the village preschool playgroup met in our room in the mornings, which meant it had a wonderful array of toys and equipment that we were allowed to use.

The children had been chosen for the enrichment group because they all had special needs and came from low-income, mostly single-parent families who were struggling to care for them. During the hour, I normally did one focused 'enrichment activity', then either a song or some nursery rhymes, and finished with a story.

On this particular day, we were going to make play dough from a simple recipe of flour, salt, water and vegetable oil. For the story I was reading *Alfie's Feet*, a tale about a little boy and his new pair of rain boots by the wonderful children's author and illustrator Shirley Hughes. I was confident Eloise could cope with these two activities, even if she had had no previous experience working with children.

First came the initial mixing of the ingredients to make the play dough, which I did, because boiling water was involved. Once it had cooled down, I then divided it up among the children. They would each choose a colour to mix into it and do the final kneading themselves. They were then free to use their imagination to make something, which they could take home.

Handing the different food-colouring gels to Eloise, I asked her to go from child to child, dispensing the colour each one requested.

We immediately ran into problems. Eloise wasn't exaggerating her difficulty with Welsh, because despite having been in the Welsh education system all her life, she was unable to recognize the words '*coch*' – red – and '*glas*' – blue – when the children said them, and thus started a constant, rather whiny, 'What's he saying?' 'I don't understand,' 'I don't know.'

And then she got to Buddug.

Buddug was five, making her the youngest in the group. She was a big girl for her age, what we would have called 'husky' in my day, so it was easy to forget she was as young as she was. Her clothes were never quite appropriate, but not in that sweet five-year-old-dressing-herself sort of way. Buddug's wardrobe had more of a charity-box vibe as everything had been over-washed and nothing really fitted, especially over her chubby tummy. Add to this a curly mass of startlingly red hair that never stayed in a ponytail, and pale, pale Celtic skin, and you had a child that you didn't forget easily.

No one seemed to know what precisely was wrong with Buddug. She was unable to talk due to what was thought to be a physiological impairment. Instead, she made an open-mouthed hissy sound or sharp, machine-gun-like grunts. These noises covered all communication. Coupled with this, she was very shy. I suspect this was mostly due to not yet having the tools to cope with her disability and thus she simply avoided interacting, if she could. Sadly, she came from a deeply impoverished single-parent family with several other siblings, who'd only recently been housed after more than a year of homelessness, so she had no one advocating her case for assessment.

The expression on Buddug's face told me that she didn't understand what we were doing. She kept glancing at the other children, trying to follow their actions, but when Eloise came to her and asked her what colour she wanted, her mouth dropped open and she stared blankly.

I came over. *'Pa liw 't ti eisiau?'*

Buddug put her hands over her face.

I took the red and the yellow gels from Eloise and held them out. 'Which one, *cariad*? Red? Or yellow?'

For a long moment Buddug did nothing. Then she slowly pointed to the yellow. I handed it to Eloise. 'Give her this one.'

Once all the children were occupied with their play dough, I handed the remaining glob to Eloise and asked her to knead colour into it. She wouldn't take it at first. When I insisted, she held it with just her fingertips. 'Which colour?' she asked, her expression pained. 'Any colour,' I said, 'you choose.' She didn't want to do it. I explained that I wanted a choice of colours, so that everyone could have two different ones to take home at the end of the session, so would she please mix colour into the remaining amount. I then left her to go around to each child to see how they were doing. When I returned to Eloise, she was still sitting, staring at the dough.

At storytime, the children gathered on the rug and I encouraged Eloise to sit with them. Bryn, who had Down's syndrome, was our charmer. Aged six, with brown, floppy hair and a gap-toothed smile, Bryn had never met a person he didn't like. When Eloise sat down on the rug, Bryn threw his arms around her. 'You're beautiful!' he said cheerfully. Eloise looked stricken.

'It's all right to ask the children to move, if they are too close,' I said.

Eloise remained frozen.

'Bryn, that's a lovely cuddle you're giving Eloise, but why don't you come up here now and sit with Rhian?' I said, indicating a spot beside me. He let go of Eloise and ran up.

I encouraged the children to act out parts of the story as I read it. The main character, Alfie, had a pair of new wellies, and stomped around in rain puddles. The children chimed in noisily with 'Splish, splash, SPLOSH!' as I read it, and they ran stomping around the room. This was too much for Eloise. She retreated to the back table.

I could feel Eloise's exhaustion when we got into the car to go home.

'What did you think of that?' I asked.

Eloise let out a long breath. 'I was expecting it to be like that group you had at Harewood,' she said, 'but this one was way harder.'

'How so?'

'I don't know.'

'Did you find it overwhelming?' I asked, hoping to give her a name to the feeling.

'I don't know.'

'It's okay to feel that way. First days are always a little over-whelming, just because everything is so new. Things'll get better as you get more used to it.'

Then silence. Several minutes passed with Eloise watching the scenery along her side of the car.

'I don't like that one little girl,' she said at last.

'Which one was that?'

'The one with the frizzy red hair.'

'Do you mean Buddug?'

'That's such a weird name.'

'It's the Welsh version of Victoria.'

'It doesn't sound *anything* like Victoria.'

'No, because it's in Welsh. The word is related to the Celtic name Boudicca. You know, the famous warrior queen who took on the Romans.'

'I think it's ugly.'

I didn't reply.

'I don't like her.'

'Why is that?'

'I don't know. I just don't. I wish she wasn't in the group.'

The next Wednesday, Eloise was waiting for me at the school bus stop. Her face brightened and she waved when she recognized my car pulling up.

'You look in a good mood,' I said.

Eloise was smiling as she got in. 'I am!'

'Are you looking forward to Pen-y-Garth?' I asked hopefully.

'Yes, I think I am,' she said. 'I even told my teacher about it.'

'Which teacher is this?'

'Mrs Morris. My domestic science teacher. We were doing these Rice Krispie treat things, and I told her I was helping you. Because I was thinking that maybe sometime we could make those at Pen-y-Garth. You can squish the Rice Krispie stuff into shapes just like play dough. We could do it and then when the kids wanted, they could *eat* it!'

'That's a very cool idea, Eloise. I really like that.'

'And *I* could eat it,' she said mischievously. 'I want to make a whole pan of that just for myself.'

I laughed.

'But you know what? When I told Mrs Morris that I thought it would be fun for the children, the first thing she said was, "You shouldn't do that, because you'd have to be so careful not to burn the little ones. The mixture is very hot when it comes off the cooker."' Eloise snorted. 'As if I wouldn't know that myself.'

'She's just being cautious. I think all teachers are like that.'

'I still think it's a good idea. We could be careful enough. We were last week and you used boiling water.'

'We have a bigger problem,' I said, 'and that's that we don't have a cooker available to us.'

'Oh. I didn't think of that,' she said in a deflated voice.

'That's okay. It was still a very good idea. We might still be able to adapt it at some point.'

We rode a few miles in silence.

'This has been such a crap week,' she said, her head turned away from me as she watched the scenery.

'How so?' I asked.

'Olivia is unwell, for one thing.'

'Oh?'

'She's got food poisoning. She's so, so sick.'

'I'm sorry to hear that,' I said. 'Food poisoning can be very unpleasant.'

'It was from mayonnaise. From a ham sandwich with mayonnaise. If you leave things with mayonnaise in them out in a place that's too warm, it can make you horribly sick.'

'Yes, that's true,' I replied. My antennae went up. While she had prefaced the conversation with a weary comment about how this had been a crap week, there was a subtle change in mood as she started to talk of the food poisoning. Eloise didn't sound particularly concerned for her friend. Indeed, her tone was more what you'd expect when someone has juicy gossip.

'Olivia was on a camping trip and they had made all the sandwiches and left them out on the picnic table. That's how it happened. A bad sandwich, and it's frightened Olivia so much. She hates to be poorly. She's nervous that way and gets dreadfully upset when she's sick, but I've said not to worry. Food poisoning is horrid, but you get over it. I've had to take care of her. When she was puking, I held back her hair for her. Then I got a cool cloth to put on her forehead to help her feel better. She's almost over it, but it's made for a hard week. I'm quite tired.'

I honestly didn't know what to make of this. The story itself sounded fishy to me, and I was still unclear about the Olivia/Heddwen dichotomy. Was this Heddwen she was talking about? I couldn't imagine Eloise would have been allowed anywhere near her. Was this a real event with imaginary characters? Or an imaginary event with real characters? Or just plain made up altogether? Or could she be telling me about something that had really happened? Was Olivia Heddwen? Or was Olivia someone else entirely?

'Food poisoning lasts about five days,' Eloise continued. 'You're not puking the whole time, but you feel vile. It takes a while to get your strength back.'

'It sounds like you're speaking from experience,' I said. 'Have you had food poisoning yourself?'

'No, but my mum used to get it all the time, because she never paid attention to what she was doing with food. I had to take care of her every single time. I had to carry the puke pots and empty them. I'm the one who made certain she *had* puke pots. Darren wouldn't have, that's for certain. That was her boyfriend. He was as useless as a chocolate teapot.'

'You were very little in those days to have that kind of responsibility.'

'Yes,' Eloise said, her tone casual. 'But somebody had to be the responsible one. My mum sure never was. That's why it's so stupid what Mrs Morris said to me about the cooker, because I've been using a cooker since I was, like, five. A gas one, too. I even had to light it. That's because I always had to get us something to eat. You wouldn't believe how many times there wasn't any food in the house because my mum and Darren were high someplace and didn't come home. I used to go to McDonald's and steal packets of ketchup to eat. Did you know that if you put ketchup on crisps, it makes them taste like you have chips?'

There was a sudden pause, the sort that follows sharing too much information. Eloise brought her hand up to cover her mouth for a moment. Then she said in a gentler tone, 'She didn't mean to. I know Mum didn't mean to. It made me mad, because I never got to do stuff like other kids, but I know it was just the drink and stuff. Those things are like a disease. Once they get hold of you, you're a different person and you forget who you're supposed to love.'

'You had a tough time,' I said. 'Both you and your mum had a tough time.'

'I worry about her sometimes,' Eloise said softly. 'I wish the social workers would let me talk to her, even if it was just, like, at Christmas or something, because lots of times, I'm wondering how she's getting on. But she lost her rights to me and isn't supposed to contact me, so I'll never know.'

'That must be hard on both of you.'

She nodded. 'Yes, it is.'

chapter nine

The most direct route to Pen-y-Garth was via a series of tiny, narrow lanes that went straight up into the hills, rather than following the A road that wound along the river in the valley. This gave us sweeping vistas over open moorland and, along one stretch, there was a breathtaking view of Snowdonia. No matter how often you saw them, the mountains never looked the same twice. The slanting light, the shifting shadows, the mist all wove their unique magic.

Eloise enjoyed the drive and often remarked on the beauty as we crested the hill that gave way to the panoramic view. 'It's so nice up here,' she said one afternoon. 'Someday, when I have a car, I'm going to drive up here all the time. I wish I could live up here.' She laughed suddenly. 'Maybe I should be a shepherd!'

A minute or two elapsed and then she said, 'Olivia loves the mountains. She's planning to live in Snowdonia. To get one of those little cottages, like the Ugly House. Do you know where that is? Have you seen it? Have you been there?'

Eloise was referring to a tiny Welsh cottage in the national park. Built in the 1400s from grey, rough-hewn stone, it had such a gnarled fairy-tale appearance that it had become a tourist attraction.

'I haven't been inside it, but I've driven by,' I replied.

'Me and Olivia, we're going to buy a cottage like that someday. I know you could probably never have that one, because it's famous, but there are other ones. There's a special back road you can take. It starts at this tea shop with lots of vines on it. My other foster parents used to take me there in the summer, because there's a lake to go swimming in, but if you don't turn off at the lake but keep driving, you come out at the Ugly House. Along the way, there's all these other old cottages, just like the Ugly House. And they're by themselves and it's so beautiful there. Me and Olivia are going to buy one someday and fix it up. We might have animals. I want chickens. I like chickens.'

Eloise was smiling to herself, her eyes fixed on the distance. The mountains had disappeared behind the tilt of the hill but she gazed onward as if they were still there.

'Some people like the sea,' Eloise said. 'They always want to be by the seaside. If it's a holiday, they're like, I want to go to Blackpool or somewhere like Madeira, where it's hot and there's sand and sea. But not me, and not Olivia either. We like the mountains best.' She looked over. 'You're like that too, aren't you? Because you've got your little farm in the hills. You're not going to end up in some seaside bungalow when you retire.'

I smiled. 'I'm not retiring quite yet.'

'You're old.'

'Not quite *that* old,' and I grinned. 'But yes, you're right. The mountains for me too.'

'Yep,' she said. 'Mountains are best.'

I was still trying to decode Olivia. I'd initially believed she was a fantasy version of Heddwen, but as Eloise chatted I began to have a gut feeling that something more was going on. The food poisoning episode seemed odd to me. Sue-Pugh had said nothing about Eloise bothering the Powells recently, nor had she mentioned Heddwen being unwell. This made it more likely that Eloise had made the story up. My uncertainty was further aroused with this mountain conversation, because hadn't Eloise originally told me that Heddwen wanted to be a marine biologist? That wouldn't be a compatible job for someone who hoped to live in the mountains.

I found it challenging to know how best to proceed with the Olivia information. Enquiring directly simply shut Eloise down, yet I felt Olivia was an important part of understanding what was going on between Heddwen and Eloise, so I wanted to keep her talking.

Since Eloise had brought Olivia into the conversation spontaneously, it felt appropriate to continue. So I asked, 'Have you given the ring back to Olivia yet?'

This sudden change of direction in the conversation caught Eloise off guard. She looked over, her brow furrowed, and there was a long pause, which may have been appraising – in other words, Eloise was trying to figure out what I was after in asking that. Or, more mundanely, she may simply have needed time to think of an answer. When she replied, it was in a cautious voice. 'No. Olivia said I could keep it.'

I found this an interesting response. Returning the ring to Olivia was the original reason Eloise had given for asking me to help her, so I would have expected her to tell me when the matter had been resolved. She'd never mentioned it. Either this meant she was keeping the information from me to ensure I continued working with her, or, more likely, that the episode with the ring had been made up and she'd simply forgotten about it.

'So the ring is no longer an issue?' I asked.

Suddenly Eloise seemed to realize the implausibility of her storyline. Her cheeks reddened. 'Are you pissed off with me?' she asked.

'No, just wondering.'

Eloise opened her handbag and rooted through the contents. Out came a tissue which she opened to reveal the ring. Slipping it on her finger, she held it up for me to see. 'Look, it's right here. Olivia understands I didn't steal it. She's forgiven me.'

'Okay. Very well. I'm glad it's sorted.'

'Are you pissed off?' she asked again.

'No. I am surprised though, because you went to a lot of trouble to find me that first time, and you told me then it was because of this ring.'

A long pause followed. Eloise shifted in her seat, pulling out the shoulder strap of the seat belt where it crossed over her chest, as if it were choking her. Then she said in a small voice, 'Do you still want to help me, even if I don't have to give the ring back any more?'

'Do you still want me to help you?'

She nodded. 'Yes, I do.'

'Then yes, I think we're good.'

The children were always touchingly pleased to see Eloise. When we arrived that afternoon, Ffion grabbed her arm and launched into a convoluted story about her baby brother, known to us all simply as Baban Bach, which meant 'little baby' in Welsh. Two of the other girls trailed behind, giggling, as Ffion dragged Eloise towards the chairs.

Eloise was still hesitant to interact freely with the children but she was growing less fearful of them. Ffion was a useful ally in this because she was such an extrovert. When I'd first started with the Pen-y-Garth group I'd found Ffion crazy-making, because she was the kind of child always wanting to hang all over you, pulling at your clothes, clinging to your arms, patting your head and face, and she would just never, ever stop chattering, no matter what. This was, however, perhaps what Eloise needed, this well-intentioned, insistent preferencing, because the hour would start with Ffion hanging on her, holding her hand, locking arms with her and chattering away, completely unbothered that Eloise may or may not have been making sense of her half-English, half-Welsh conversation. I noticed by the end of today's session that Eloise was smiling at Ffion and beckoning for her to sit beside her.

We had a rowdy time that day, acting out nursery rhymes, singing and dancing, so at the end of the hour I opted to do a relaxing visualization to calm the group down.

'Find a space to stand. Everyone in their own place, please. Bryn, move over. Lewis doesn't need help. Okay, ready? Okay? I want you to close your eyes.'

I glanced around the group. 'Buddug, close your eyes, please.' I touched my eyes. '*Cau dy llygaid.*'

She stared blankly at me. I looked at the others. Everyone else was standing, eyes closed, including Eloise. Ffion had moved over to hang on Eloise's arm.

I let Buddug be, hoping she'd join in as we got started.

'Imagine you're a snowman. Where have you been built? Maybe you are a snowman in your front garden. Or the back garden. Maybe in the park. It doesn't matter. It's snowing and there is plenty of space around. Take a moment to imagine yourself as a big, white snowman. In your mind's eye, see the group of children who are building you. First, they roll a big, big snowball for your bottom, and then they roll a medium-sized snowball for your tummy, and ooph, lift it up. Then a smaller snowball for your head. What have they used to make your eyes? Are they pieces of coal? Or stones? Or something else? And what about your nose? Is it a carrot? And your mouth?'

'My eyes are made from chestnuts!' Bethan said. This, of course, caused several others to say what their eyes and nose were made of before I could get them focused back on the visualization.

'You are standing straight and tall. A straight and tall snowman.'

'My arms are sticking out like this, because they are just

sticks,' Lewis interjected, putting his arms out. 'So they stick out.' He laughed at this wordplay.

'Yes, good, Lewis, keep your eyes closed, please. And let's see you being a tall, straight, newly built snowman.'

I glanced at Eloise, who stood straight and tall, like the children. It pleased me to see her participating, and that she did not feel the teenager so much that she was worried about looking silly.

'And now . . .' I said, 'the sun is coming out. It is a beautiful day with a bright blue sky and a nice warm sun. It's getting warmer and warmer. What starts to happen to you?'

'I dance!' shouted Katie, and she began to dance joyfully around the room. This meant, of course, that several others started to dance too.

'Katie, you're a snowman, all straight and tall. Not a dancing snowman, because you don't have any legs, do you? Everyone else? You don't have legs! So stand straight and tall, please. And listen to what I've said. The sun comes out and it gets warmer and warmer. What happens to a snowman then?'

'He melts.' This was Eloise, and I think she was as surprised to find herself answering as I was. Her eyes popped open and she covered her mouth in embarrassment. I grinned.

'That's right. Snowmen melt in the bright sunshine, and that's what I want you to do. Slowly, slowly melt. First your head begins to thaw. Feel the warm sun on your head. Feel your head going all soft and slushy. And then your arms begin to droop . . .'

I carried on describing the melting snowman, part by part. Most of the children were following this well and pretending to melt down to the ground, but not Buddug. She had never closed her eyes at all during the exercise, and as I spoke, she watched me, her brow furrowed. I regretted not being able to do this in Welsh, because the English was no doubt making it harder for her to figure out the activity. '*Dwt ti'n toddi*,' I said – telling her to melt – but I didn't know the word for 'pretend', so I wasn't sure if her expression of confusion was due to not understanding my Welsh or understanding me fine but having no clue why I wanted her to melt.

The other children were soon relaxed puddles on the floor and started to open their eyes. Eloise had melted a little bit but kept her composure enough not to end up on the floor. Ffion, busybody that she was, was quick to notice Buddug still standing. Going over, she spoke a flurry of Welsh and pushed Buddug's shoulders down to force her to the floor. Buddug resisted this and broke away with a squeal.

'She's *twp*, Miss. She won't do it,' Ffion announced.

'Please don't say that. We don't call people names in here,' I said. 'And it doesn't matter if Buddug doesn't want to do it. It's just for fun. To make us feel nice and relaxed before we go home. So let's get our things on now, and go look for Mum or Dad.'

'Or *Nain*,' Ffion shouted. '*Daw fy nain!*'

'Okay, yes, mums, dads, *nains*, childminders, whoever usually comes to pick you up after group.'

The usual chaos of trying to get young children into rain gear ensued and then the sudden whoosh of silence when the last one was out the door.

I stuck my tongue out in a gesture of exhaustion as I came back into the room to gather together my belongings.

'Yes, I'm all melted out,' Eloise said, with a gleam in her eye.

A small smile came across her lips. 'I noticed a little kitchen by the back door where you go out to the loos,' she said. 'Could we have a cuppa before we go back?' She opened her bag. 'I brought us teabags. *And* milk!'

As we sat, nursing our cups of tea, Eloise said, 'So what's wrong with that Buddug girl?'

'She has developmental delay.'

'You mean she's retarded,' Eloise said.

'That's not a helpful word to describe people.'

'Yes, well, even I know what "*twp*" means, and it's pretty hard not to notice Buddug's not with the show.'

'Buddug comes from a very difficult background, and to add to it she has a genetic issue the doctors don't seem to know much about, so she's struggling a bit at this time.'

'Oh, come off it. Buddug didn't even know how to pretend to be a snowman,' Eloise said dismissively.

'It doesn't matter. She'll come on when she's ready.'

'The other kids don't like her. They think she's weird. I have to stop them bullying her when you're not looking. Bethan spat on Buddug when the girls were out in the toilet block.'

'I hope you stopped that straightaway.'

'Yes, of course I did,' she said in an offended voice. 'What did you think I'd do? Spit too?'

A pause came then. Eloise looked around the small kitchen in a random way, then back at me.

'She reminds me of my sister.'

'Buddug?'

'My sister was ginger like that and really curly. Mum used those same kind of ponytail holders Buddug has. I think that hairstyle is so ugly. And that girl has hardly any hair, so they're like two blobs of red fuzz. They make her look *twp*, even without saying it.'

'You were saying the other time you don't like her and didn't know why. Do you think that's perhaps why you have such strong feelings?' I asked. 'The fact she reminds you of your sister?'

'*No*,' Eloise said indignantly.

A pause.

'My sister didn't have "developmental delay". She would have been able to do that snowman thing, no trouble, and she was only three.'

'Sometimes our feelings carry over from one person to another because we've had a bad association. For instance, when I first started teaching, I had a little boy named Gavin in my class who was really, really naughty. So, for quite a while, whenever I met a boy named Gavin I struggled to like him, because I associated the name with someone who was badly behaved.'

Eloise looked at me with disgust. 'Crap, I'm glad you're not my teacher, if you get influenced easily as that. The poor other Gavins couldn't help having the name of someone you didn't like long ago,' Eloise replied.

I didn't mention that this was my point.

Eloise humphed again. 'Anyway, that's not true for me. My sister's name is Evie, so I'm not doing what you just said.'

chapter ten

Each Wednesday Eloise came with me to the enrichment group at Pen-y-Garth. While she didn't take naturally to working with the children, she was clearly enjoying our car rides back and forth and it was during this time we were able to have our most enjoyable conversations. This wasn't the same as saying they were full of deep or heartfelt psychological insight. Eloise was a master at keeping things at a casual level, so we talked mostly about soap operas, reality stars and make-up. In the same way that she enjoyed making tea, Eloise enjoyed these conversations. They were what she looked forward to, and I did too. I'd grown to love her quiet personality and dry sense of humour.

Eloise slowly warmed to Ffion, possibly because Ffion really, really, *really* liked her and was totally undisguised in her admiration for everything Eloise did. Eloise had something of an obsession with nail varnish. She loved to try out different colours and found a most appreciative audience in Ffion, who was desperate each week to see what Eloise was wearing.

Eloise was also very kind to Rhian, who had dyspraxia. This caused her movements to be large and clumsy, and gave rise to a speech impediment that made Rhian self-conscious. Eloise noticed her reluctance to participate in the group and was good at ensuring Rhian wasn't overlooked and coaxing her to join in.

The activities I chose each week for the group continued to bemuse Eloise. She always participated, but could never quite let go of her self-consciousness, so her actions were always stilted, as if she were acting out a part. I couldn't tell if this was a reflection of her abusive childhood when there had been little time for childish activities, or if she was simply showing normal adolescent concern about looking silly.

The cup of tea afterwards became our weekly ritual. Eloise enjoyed every aspect of it, from bringing the items to brewing it, serving it and the fifteen minutes or so we then took to drink it. While we drank our tea we chatted, usually about the session we'd just finished, but always light-heartedly. Eloise would laugh and recount funny things the children had done. Occasionally she would ask for clarification of an activity, if there was something she didn't quite understand, but it was all small talk. I toyed with the idea that this, itself – the very ordinariness of sharing a chat and cup of tea – may have been why it was such a powerful experience for Eloise. 'Ordinary', particularly when one on one with a safe adult, must have been a precious commodity in Eloise's world. It crossed my mind that 'ordinary' might actually be our therapy.

During these conversations, two topics never came up. The first was Heddwen. Throughout my entire time working with Eloise, she had never mentioned Heddwen spontaneously. This seemed curious to me, given how much space Heddwen Powell must have occupied in Eloise's head. I was hoping, however, that lack of reference was an indication the obsession was starting to wane. During the time she had been going with me to Pen-y-Garth, Eloise had not gone to the Powells' once. Three, four, five weeks went by. Her behaviour began to improve in other areas concordantly. Sue-Pugh phoned, delighted to tell me that Eloise had been going to school regularly, attending classes and not truanting, and she had not run away from home for more than six weeks.

The other topic to disappear was Olivia. We'd had those two conversations in the car – the one on food poisoning and the one on the ring – and that was it. Eloise didn't mention Olivia again. This left me more convinced than ever that Heddwen and Olivia were the same person, that Olivia was perhaps a fantasized version of Heddwen, and as Eloise's interest in Heddwen waned, so did it in Olivia.

Of course, I could have asked her directly about either topic, but this wasn't my way. Now that we had time and I was no longer restricted to getting information out of Eloise in six sessions, my instinct was to leave all the information-giving in Eloise's court. This allowed her control of what we talked about, which I hoped would eventually make her more comfortable with trusting me. Just as important, however, was letting Eloise guide the topics which allowed me to see the 'landscape' of our conversations – how various subjects came up, when they came up, the manner in which Eloise developed them. This gave me insight into her thought processes, how she prioritized things and, to a degree, how she problem-solved.

Spring arrived. With it came the most labour-intensive period on the farming calendar: lambing. I kept a flock of sixty pedigreed Black Welsh Mountain sheep, which are a small, wiry, fairly primitive breed that do well in the wet, mountainous Welsh countryside, and the month of April was all about birth.

To people not closely bound to the land, it's hard to imagine how the arrival of fluffy little lambs can be the intense, twenty-four-hour, seven-day-a-week process it is, but on sheep farms all over the nation, life comes to a complete halt for six weeks in the spring. You do nothing but schlep back and forth to the barn twenty-four hours a day to check on everyone, because the line between life and death can be perilously thin during those weeks. If necessary, you 'pull' lambs, easing them out of their mothers because, for one reason or another, they can't manage it themselves. You see them to their feet, help with finding a nice, milky teat under tangles of fleece and occasionally have to convince an unwilling mother that that little wet, squirmy bundle is indeed her infant and she'd better take care of it. If you are unlucky she refuses to take your word for it, and you end up boiling water and mixing infant lamb formula (because, yes, there is such a thing) and then spending the wee hours cajoling a newborn to take a bottle it doesn't want. Only very occasionally do you sleep.

As a consequence, the enrichment group did not meet for those few weeks. This was normal and expected. We lived in a rural area where almost everyone was involved in one aspect or another of sheep farming, so we were all lambing. Even if I hadn't needed the time off myself, it was likely that many of the children's families would have been too busy with lambing to bring the kids in. So no group. I had warned Eloise numerous times about this, and she assured me that it was no problem, that she understood why I'd be away and would look forward to resuming in early May.

By late April, most of my sheep had given birth, so lambing had transitioned into caring for the pet lambs, the ones who could not be reared by their mother. In my case, most were the third lamb from sets of triplets. Ewes have only two teats, so when they give birth to three lambs it is difficult for them to feed all three properly and the weakest one dies. This is especially true among mountain sheep who live on poor grazing land. As a consequence, when triplets occur the farmer typically takes the weakest lamb off the ewe and bottle-feeds it to ensure its survival. In the beginning this is labour-intensive, because young lambs have small tummies and need feeding every four hours, but once they are fed they go to sleep, and there is usually a decent block of time to do other things.

The weather was lovely the whole month of April, so after I finished with the pet lambs one day, I went out to the vegetable garden to turn over the soil in preparation for planting potatoes.

Our house and farm buildings were down a lengthy private drive with hedgerows on either side. The vegetable garden was along one side of this drive, so that's where I was with my garden fork when I became aware of someone on the other side of the hedgerow, walking along our drive from the road. This was unusual. We were in the middle of nowhere, so pedestrians were pretty much non-existent.

As it was mid-morning, my husband was at work and my daughter at school, which meant I was home alone in the vegetable garden, except for my Labrador Mickey, so I was a little disconcerted to hear someone on foot. The hedgerow made it impossible to see who was there, so I went down through the garden gate beside the barn, bringing Mickey with me, just in case he might morph from the wimp that he was into a Rottweiler.

Eloise.

She smiled cheerfully when she saw me, as if this were the most normal of meetings. 'I thought I'd come and visit you,' she said. 'It's been, like, ages. Can I see your lambs?'

'How did you get up here?' I asked.

'The bus,' she replied brightly.

'The nearest bus stop is three miles from here.'

'Yes, I know. So I walked,' she said, as if I were being terribly dense for asking. 'I've been here before, remember? And it is daytime now, because last time you got pissy about me coming at night.' There was a puppy-dog quality to her tone of voice. I could hear how pleased she was with herself for being a good girl and following my previous advice.

'Shouldn't you be in school today?'

She shrugged casually, then gestured off beyond me. 'I love all those daffodils you've got.'

Part of me wanted to respond in kind to Eloise's bubbly demeanour. She seemed so pleased to see me, to be up here in the sunshine and beautiful surroundings. It would be fun to show her the garden, to take her around the farm, to let her bottle-feed a lamb. Another part of me wanted to do nothing of the sort, because this was wrong on so many levels. Her non-chalant acknowledgement that she'd bunked off school told me not only that she didn't take the truancy seriously but that she also didn't expect me to. More than that was the whole issue of turning up at my house unexpectedly. This was inappropriate, which I apparently hadn't communicated clearly enough the previous time she'd shown up. It wasn't just the safety issue of walking long distances alone along country roads. It was also about crossing a fairly serious boundary. Just as it was not appropriate that she turn up at the Powells' uninvited, it was not appropriate that she turn up at my house. I did not want to reward her for it.

'Is that your daughter's bike?' Eloise asked, pointing across the yard.

'Let me get cleaned up, and I'll take you back down to school.'

'Can I see inside your house?'

'Eloise, listen—'

'Is that your daughter's swing set?'

'Eloise, listen to me. We're getting in the car and I'll take you back down.'

She reached out to pet Mickey. 'What's your dog's name?'

'*Listen*. No. We're not doing this. It isn't appropriate just to turn up here, just like it isn't appropriate to turn up at the Powells'. I'm sorry.'

A sudden, stricken look as understanding dawned on her. The way her expression changed, it was as if I had stabbed her.

'*Jesus!* All I wanted to know was your dog's name. That's all I asked,' she said piteously. 'What's wrong with that?' And before I could respond, she turned abruptly and took off, running full tilt down the drive towards the road.

I ran after her but stopped after a hundred metres or so, realizing that my clumsy wellies were going to trip me if I kept going. I needed to take the car to catch her, but dropping everything to chase down Eloise wasn't quite such a simple thing. My young daughter was due home shortly from primary school, and the pet lambs were already bleating in the barn for their next feed. Knowing I would need to talk with Eloise once I caught up with her, and I'd then have to get her safely home, I had to make arrangements before I could take off.

Fortunately, my father-in-law lived with us. Unfortunately, he was ninety-seven. While he was a fit, alert man for his age, and would be more than happy to meet the school bus and feed the lambs for me, I knew he wouldn't be able to cope with the detailed instructions for making up the lambs' milk and putting the right portions into sterilized bottles, so I needed to do that myself before I could leave.

Fifteen minutes passed before I was able to get into the car to go look for Eloise. I was pretty sure she would have headed back towards the village where the bus stop was, and I hoped she hadn't got there yet. So it was. I came across her walking along the verge of the road about a mile and a half from the house.

Eloise ignored me when I pulled abreast of her. Rolling down the window, I called for her to get in the car. She kept walking. I drove the car up onto the verge, blocking her way.

'Get in, please,' I said.

She endeavoured to get past me but, in the narrow lane, there wasn't enough room between my bumper and the hedgerow.

'Eloise, get in. Come on. I mean it. Get in.'

Shaking her head, she began to cry.

'This is a very small road, Eloise, and another car could come up over the hill at any moment. They're not going to expect someone blocking the lane like this. You could get badly hurt. We both could. So get in. Now.'

A long moment's hesitation and Eloise finally opened my car door, although she got into the back seat, not into the passenger seat next to me. I pressed the child lock.

Heading down the lane towards the village, I looked at her in the rear-view mirror. 'Listen, kiddo, I'm sorry how this played out. I know what I said must have sounded like I don't want to see you and that isn't true. I am happy to see you. But this just isn't the appropriate way to go about it.'

She continued crying.

What I was saying wasn't coming out right. The more I tried to explain what the problem was, the more complicated I made it sound and the harder Eloise cried. My initial intention had been to take her back to her school, but I was reluctant to leave her in her current state. Eloise was too much of an escape artist, but more than that, it felt important to take the time to listen to her, or at least give her the chance to be listened to. I'd reached the main coast road by this point, a big dual carriageway, and on one side was a roadside cafe. I crossed over and pulled into the car park.

'Let's have a cuppa,' I said.

'I don't want to.'

'No, maybe not. But I do,' I said, and got out of the car. I waited beside the back door until Eloise got out as well, because I didn't want to risk her running off.

Inside, I chose a booth by the window and ordered us a round of teacakes and a pot of tea. Eloise slouched down in her seat. She had stopped crying but her eyes were red and puffy and this embarrassed her. She kept her hand up when the waitress brought over our food. Sitting back, I gave her a chance to be 'mother', lingo for being the person who stirred the pot and poured the tea, but Eloise was having none of it, and none of her teacake either, which she shoved away. I stirred the pot, added milk to our cups and poured. Then I sat back and turned my attention to buttering my teacake.

'Why are you doing this?' she asked.

'Doing what?'

'This. *This*. You're making fun of me.'

Surprised, I looked over. 'No, I'm not. I stopped here because I thought we could do with a bit of time to talk. And that refreshments would help. How does it feel like I'm making fun of you?'

'Because you are.'

'Eloise, I'm not. I promise. This is just a cup of tea and a tea-cake. There's no other meaning to it.'

'I'm not eating it,' she said, and shoved the plate with the teacake further away from her.

'That's all right. You can choose.'

'*See?*' she cried. 'You're making fun of me.'

I was madly scrambling to interpret what was going on. It wasn't at all clear to me how we had got from my saying it was inappropriate to turn up uninvited at my house to my 'making fun' of her by buying her a teacake. I could understand her being upset at my setting boundaries but we seemed to have moved past that to something equally, if not more, upsetting.

'I'm sorry that we haven't had much time together lately. I've missed you too. And I'm sorry how things worked out at the house. So I thought we needed a chance to talk to each other,' I said. 'That's why I stopped here. That's the only reason. I'm not trying to make you feel bad. I'm not making fun of you. And I thought a cup of tea would be nice.'

'And I said I don't *want* it,' she muttered.

'I'd like to talk about what happened up at the house, because it may have felt like rejection. That isn't true, so I'd like us to discuss it. I'm sensing we have something else going on too, because suddenly the tea and the teacake have become a big deal. So I'm wondering if it's a kind of tit-for-tat thing. I made you feel rejected and so now you want to make me feel rejected.'

'*No,*' Eloise said acridly. 'That's stupid. That is a stupid connection. Like, a five-year-old might think that way, but . . . Do you think of me like a five-year-old?'

'No. I'm just trying to understand.'

'I don't see how you got a job working with people, because you suck at it big time.'

I finished my teacake.

Eloise started to cry again. Initially a single tear ran silently over her cheek. She lowered her head and leaned forward on her fists.

I handed her a tissue.

Wiping her eyes, she looked over at me. 'You want me to say how important you are to me? You want to think your rejection matters? Well, lady, it doesn't. You're fucking small change in the rejection department, because my mum rejected me and my dad rejected me and my gran rejected me, so I'm a rejection professional. I get strong on rejection. I'm not crying about you. I'm crying because I'm just so pissed off I can hardly stand it.'

That much, I realized, was probably true.

Several moments of uncomfortable silence passed. The aura of unfinished business was almost palpable. I wanted to give us more time, but it was nearly five and the cafe closed then. Moreover, I'd drunk most of the tea in the teapot myself and now I needed the toilet, but I didn't dare leave her at the table alone, because I was certain she would run away.

Eloise lifted her long hair up off her shoulders and held it in a ponytail for a few moments before letting it drop. 'I won't eat that,' she said, once again indicating the contentious teacake.

'That's fine.'

'I'm just going to waste it.'

'It's okay,' I said.

She gave me a long, hard look and shook her head very slightly. 'You pretend everything's so cool. You think you're so awesome, like, you're this mega-empathetic person who understands everyone. But like I said, I've been here before. I don't get fooled by people like you, who go around sprinkling their sparkles like a fucking Disney princess.'

Her voice had grown unexpectedly soft. 'I'm just a case to you. A diagnosis, some tick boxes and a fucking big file, that's all. You don't see me. You think you do, but you don't. The truth of the matter is, I'm as invisible to you as I am to everyone else.'

chapter eleven

Eloise was right. I didn't know what it was like to be her. While I'd come from humble beginnings myself, they were privileged compared to Eloise's life. I'd always known love, security and enough food on the table. I had no idea what Eloise's degree of disenfranchisement must have felt like.

On the other hand, Eloise was also wrong. Although they can start out feeling equally painful, there is a distinct difference between rejection and having boundaries set. She had grown up in an environment where there had been few appropriate boundaries. Eloise had often been the adult, even as a preschooler, nursing her mother through her bouts of drinking and depression, but her mother had not nurtured Eloise or kept her safe in return. Eloise's father couldn't stay clean and out of prison long enough to maintain any relationship with her, and her stepfather Darren had exploited her sexually before she'd even reached adolescence. How was she to know how healthy relationships worked? Barging in on people to demand attention had been a pragmatic approach to getting her needs met with the dysfunctional adults in her life. I realized that appropriately set boundaries were going to feel painfully similar to rejection to someone used to none at all.

From the roadside cafe, I drove Eloise back to her foster home. She was still angry with me and did not speak the entire journey. I let her be. Pulling into the drive, I said, 'I'm back with the group next Wednesday. I'll see you then.'

Leaping from the car the moment it stopped, Eloise slammed the door without looking back. I stayed in the drive until she went inside.

Returning to the farm, I mulled the afternoon's events over. While considering Eloise's history of inappropriate or non-existent boundaries, I began to wonder about her fixation with Heddwen. Given her complicated history of sexual abuse in early childhood, it would not be surprising if Eloise exhibited over-sexualized behaviour at fourteen, but thus far, no one had observed this happening. While Eloise clearly had a crush on Heddwen, same-sex crushes are a normal part of being fourteen. She had not verbalized any romantic or sexual intentions towards Heddwen.

This made me wonder if her fixation might be less a case of stalking and more an issue of misunderstanding boundaries. A need for connection seemed to build up to the point that Eloise felt compelled to act on it. I'd seen this on the three different occasions when she had barged in on me in quite spectacular fashion without showing any signs that she understood this was inappropriate or that I might not be happy about it. Her chaotic past had left her self-sufficient. When she needed a connection, she made it happen. It wasn't a two-way street for her.

The next Wednesday I was relieved to see Eloise waiting when I came to pick her up to go to the enrichment group in Pen-y-Garth. When I'd left her the previous week, I'd felt almost certain she would act out in some way, either by running away or at the very least by avoiding me. Neither happened. Instead, she opened the car door, greeted me cheerfully and got in. However, the mood was different in the car than it usually was. Eloise was subdued, although not in a sulky way. She just sat quietly watching the scenery and didn't speak. I didn't prod her. Some things are best left to settle.

The weather hadn't got the memo about its being spring. We were into early May by that point, but there followed a seemingly endless run of cold, blustery days that brought late-season snow to the higher ground and sleet to us in the valleys. It was impossible to enjoy being outside. As a consequence, the children in the enrichment group were wildly ramped up with unused energy on that Wednesday afternoon, which made it feel as if I were trapped in a room with crazed howler monkeys.

For our main activity, the children were going to build alphabet letters from Lego. The idea was that they would make the letters of their first name, and I had created a template for each child to follow. What actually happened, however, was a lot of energetic screaming and chucking bricks at each other. After the fourth unsuccessful attempt at getting everyone focused, I realized this activity was not going to happen, so I gave up and told the children to gather in a circle on the floor.

'Who's fed up with the weather?'

'Me! Me! Me, me, me!' came the answer from every direction.

'Do you know what I think we need?' I asked with exaggerated enthusiasm. 'A holiday! Somewhere nice and sunny where everyone can run and play. Where shall we go?'

Lively possibilities were offered up. 'To *Nain*'s?' Bethan said.

'Only if your *nain* lives in Spain, Bethan.'

'To the supermarket?' Lewis offered.

'It's not sunny at the supermarket,' Katie replied.

'And is it a good idea to run and play there?' I asked.

'I know! I know! I know!' Ffion squealed. 'To London! To London! To visit the Queen!'

I smiled at her. 'You mean like the pussycat did? That's a good place. Those are all good places. But you know where I think we should go? To the beach! To a nice, warm, sunny beach where everyone can run around.'

Appreciative oohs and aahs from everyone except Buddug. Buddug was picking lint out of the rug.

'I want to go to Majorca!' Lewis said. 'There's a beach there.'

'We haven't got our suitcases with us,' Ffion replied in a dejected tone.

'We don't need suitcases where we're going,' I said, and explained that we were going to travel using our imaginations. This evoked a certain amount of scepticism, especially from Bethan, who tended to be literal on all occasions.

I asked everyone to close their eyes. Once they were all settled, I then proceeded with the visualization, describing arriving at the beach. It is a bright, sunny day. Feel how warm it is. Here we are, getting out of the car in the car park. We start down the path to the beach. Look at the ground. Is the path grassy? Are you barefoot? Can you feel the grass with your toes? Down the path we go to the beach. What colour is the sand? Can you see it stretching all along the coast? Look at the water. It's a nice bright blue, reflecting the beautiful sunny sky. You're walking on the sand now. It's very warm but not hot. Not too hot. Can you feel it? Can you feel the warm sand on your feet?

I loved doing visualizations like this. They always had such a calming effect on the children. No matter how stressed or agitated we started out, by the end of the imaginary journey even the hyperactive children had settled.

As I spun out the story of our visit to the beach, talking in detail about the tide pools with their little fish, the seaweed and crabs, the wind in our hair, I opened my eyes to see what everyone was doing. Two or three had their hands extended, feeling the invisible environment around them. Jack, who had autism, had his eyes open, but he was sitting quietly. Buddug had got up and gone to a table at the back of the room and taken a seat. She was manipulating the Lego bricks. Not building anything, just fingering through them. I could never decide if she was struggling with the second language and thus unable to follow me or if she was simply struggling. My gut feeling was the latter. As she was disturbing no one, I let her be. The other children, including Eloise, were all deeply absorbed in the visualization, their eyes closed, their attention focused.

I used almost half an hour on our imaginary trip to the beach, and when we finished, the rest of our time was spent talking about real beach trips. The children were relaxed and cheerful, and almost everyone had a story they wanted to share about where they went or what they did. It was a pleasant way to finish off the group time.

Eloise had ridden out to Pen-y-Garth in silence, the taint of our argument from the previous week still present. I thought the time in group would clear it, but Eloise was just as quiet on the way home. She kept her head turned away from me and gazed out the passenger side window, even though the low-hanging cloud meant there was no view of the mountains to be had. Indeed, it was so misty on the higher reaches of the road that we couldn't see much of anything beyond the low stone walls that ran along either side of the car.

Just as we were coming down out of the hills and approaching the main road, Eloise said, 'When you do that exercise that we did, can you actually see the beach?'

'You mean, can I visualize it in my mind? Yes, I can,' I said.

'Can you see it very clearly, as if you were right there? Like, can you see grains of sand, if you put your hand into it?'

'Yes, I can,' I said. 'I have a visual mind. I think mostly in pictures, so it's easy for me to create what I want to see. What about you? Could you see the beach?'

She pursed her lips but didn't answer.

Concerned that she may have found the visualization aspect of the exercise difficult and was feeling anxious about it, I said, 'Some people find they can't picture things in their mind, and that's perfectly normal too. They think mostly in words or sometimes just in concepts. Different minds work different ways, and one way isn't better than another.'

'Can you hear in your mind?' Eloise asked.

'Yes,' I said.

'I mean, like, do you hear words?'

'Do you mean are my thoughts in words, as if I have a commentary going on in my head?'

'No, I mean do you hear words? Like, if you were picturing everybody in the group down at the beach, could you hear them talking to each other? Them, in your mind? Or like, could you hear the seagulls?'

'Yes,' I said. 'I can. What about you?'

'Can you smell in your mind?' Eloise asked, ignoring my question. 'Like, when you were at the beach in your mind, could you smell the sea?'

'Yes,' I said. 'Could you?'

She didn't respond.

I glanced over. Eloise still had her head turned away from me. She continued to stare out the passenger side window.

'That's one of the reasons I write,' I said. 'It's like there's a whole other world inside my mind, that I can see and hear and smell, just like in the external world. I can feel it too, the sense of weight, or whether something is soft or smooth. I've got all the same senses inside my head as I do out here, so I write it down in an effort to make it real.'

'How do you mean?' she asked.

'Think of that beach in the visualization. It had all that fabulous detail – sun, a lovely cool breeze, little fish in the tide pools, warm sand between our toes – but it vanishes the moment we stop thinking about it. However, if I write it down, that fixes it in this world. Suddenly it's a real thing, on paper, and because of that I can go back to that exact beach. Each time I read the words on the paper, it exists again.'

Eloise turned her head and looked directly at me. 'Do you believe what's in your head?' she asked.

'How so?'

'Is that why you want to fix it on paper?'

I still wasn't sure I understood her question, so I asked her to elaborate.

'I mean, do you think that what you think is true? Like, is the beach real in some way, and you can see it but no one else can?'

'That's a complex question,' I replied. 'The world inside my head is real for me, but that's not the same as saying it is real as we know it out here. "Real" real.'

'But you just said you make it exist by writing about it,' Eloise said. 'You put it on paper, so that brings it into this world. You make it real, so that when someone else reads it, the world becomes real for them too. That's what you said, isn't it? That's what you meant, yes? So is it true?'

I smiled at her. 'Yes, I guess so. But there's a difference between true and real.'

'What do you mean?' Eloise asked.

We'd reached her house, so I pulled into the drive.

'Can we sit here a minute,' Eloise said, 'because I want to know your answer.'

'"Real" is this world right here that we experience with our senses. True is a concept. It means things are genuine.' I paused to gauge whether Eloise was following me, not only because we'd wandered unexpectedly into such an abstract conversation, but also because I wasn't sure I was giving very good definitions. Her expression wasn't one of confusion, however. To my surprise, this was perhaps the most fully engaged I'd seen her. She was turned in her seat, watching me carefully.

'A long time ago, when I was much younger than you are now,' I said, 'I had this huge imaginary world in my head. It started out when I was four or five with an imaginary companion called Delilah, but then Delilah had a family. Her family lived in a neighbourhood. The neighbourhood was in a village. The village was in a country, and I began to imagine more and more details of all these things. And then, as years went on, I imagined a language and a history and a religion. There was a government. There was a mythology. This went on from the time I was a little kid until I was an adult, and it became very important to me, all these people, all this stuff. When I was your age, I spent practically all my spare time developing it, writing it down, detailing it, and I had the most marvellous fun doing it.'

'Wow,' Eloise said under her breath. She tipped her head. 'So this was just in your head?'

I nodded.

'Did you ever want it to be real? Like, a real place that you could go and visit?'

I smiled. 'Yes. When I was about your age, I did. It's not easy being thirteen or fourteen and I wanted things to be different, so I began to wish I could live in Delilah's world instead of mine.'

Eloise was nodding as I spoke.

'A lot of people made me feel like I was a bit crazy for having all this world in my head,' I said. 'They didn't understand, because they didn't have anything like that experience in their own minds, so they couldn't imagine what it was like. And I couldn't imagine what it was like to be them, either. I thought they must have these big, gaping blank spots in their minds with nothing in them. I wondered how they filled their time without all this to think about. I realize now that most people are like them, not like me, but I don't think I was crazy. Just different.'

'Do you think any of it was real?' Eloise asked. 'Could your world have been like, maybe in a parallel universe or something?'

'I don't know. My definition of real has changed through the years. I don't think there's a real place somewhere that would be Delilah's world, but I do think that world has reality. It's just its own reality, and I can experience it with the senses in my mind, but it isn't this reality, so I can't experience it with the senses in my body.'

Eloise smiled. 'You are so awesome.'

I grinned.

'That is the awesomest thing anyone has ever, ever told me,' she said. Opening the car door, she got out. 'See you next Wednesday.'

chapter twelve

I went home in a great mood that afternoon. The conversation in the car was the first time I sensed that special 'click' with Eloise that signals full engagement, and as I became aware of thinking that, I realized this had been my problem all along. While Eloise professed to wanting my help and, indeed, had actively sought me out, it had never led to the kind of relationship that made me feel we were on the same team. Thus far, she had always blocked whatever I tried to do. *At last*, I was thinking as I drove over the moors towards home, *we are finally on our way*.

My sense was that Eloise's esoteric interest in reality came from what was going on inside her own head. For some while now I'd had the feeling that Eloise maintained a vivid internal life, and that this may have been spilling over into her behaviour with Heddwen Powell; that she had perhaps created an internal life where an imaginary Heddwen was responding quite differently to the real-life Heddwen, and it was this mismatch that was getting her into trouble. I hoped, by sharing the fact that I too had experience of a florid imaginary world, she would feel more comfortable revealing what was going on in her own head.

Cars are a good therapeutic milieu, in part because another activity – driving – is taking place which diffuses the intensity and limits eye contact, and in part because it is usually self-limiting insomuch as you will arrive at your destination so the conversation comes to a natural conclusion. In Eloise's case, there was the additional advantage that she couldn't escape me. Hoping to work off the connection we experienced in the car the previous Wednesday afternoon, I decided to initiate a gentle conversation about her fixation on Heddwen during our next drive to Pen-y-Garth.

'The main reason I've become involved is because of what's going on between you and the Powells,' I said, 'but, you know, we haven't talked very much about that. I know it's an uncomfortable subject, and that's one of the reasons I haven't pushed it. I'm not a very pushy person when it comes to talking about things. I'm more of a wait-and-see person, because growing and changing have their own natural pace, and I like to think topics will come up when the time is right. However, we've been doing quite a lot of waiting and seeing, and I'm not sure how much growing and changing is happening.'

'I'm okay with things like they are,' Eloise said.

'Yes, I know you are. But we can't just keep on keeping on.'

'Why not? Don't you like being with me?'

'Yes, I do like being with you. Very much. That's not the issue.'

'Don't you want to come and see me any more?' she asked in an injured voice. 'Is this you trying to stop?'

'No, it's not. Rather, it's about the fact that Sue-Pugh told me you were caught outside the Powells' last Thursday night. That's the first time you've been over there in a while, so I'm wondering what the story is.'

Eloise shrugged.

'I've heard Sue-Pugh's take on things. I'd like to hear your side of it.'

She shrugged again.

Silence.

'You know how we play that game in the enrichment group, the game with the cards where it names an emotion and then you have to describe how the emotion affects your body? For instance, if you draw the "happy" card, you talk about how the corners of your mouth go up and your eyes crinkle and look merry, and inside you start to feel good? Remember that game?'

'Yeah.'

'I want to play a version of that now.'

'I don't,' she muttered.

'No, just try it for me. Humour me.'

She huffed under her breath.

'Think about going to the Powells' house. I'm not interested in right or wrong or should or shouldn't. Instead, I want to know how it makes your body feel. Describe it to me as if it were one of those emotion cards.'

'I don't want to do that.'

'You're still hung up on thinking I'm judging. I'm not. I'm

interested in the physical sensations. That's all. I want to know what your muscles were doing.'

'No.'

'Yes.'

Then silence. So much time passed without a response that I thought I'd lost this one and she wasn't going to answer, but just when I was about to change the subject, she drew in a long breath. 'I don't know how to say it.'

'This is just a game. Say it any way it comes to you.'

'Good,' she said in almost a whisper. 'It makes me feel good. But . . . bad too . . .'

'How so?'

A long pause.

'I feel alive. When I'm there, I feel alive. Almost like I've had an upper, only better. Like my mind's woken up properly. Most of the time I feel dead. The only time I don't is when I think about Olivia.'

'And you said there's also a bad part?'

'It takes over my mind. That's the only way I can think to describe it. All I can think about is seeing Olivia. At first it feels good, but then it's like my mind starts to get exhausted. It's like one of those hamsters, you know, the kind that has a wheel in its cage and it goes around and around and around. I can't get my mind to come off. It's like when you hear really bad news. You know, shocking news, like somebody's died suddenly. You know how that takes over your mind? You can't think of anything else and you can't make yourself stop thinking about it? That's what happens. The thoughts just go around and around.

And that's why I go over there, because it's the only way to get it to stop.'

I had planned for a very silly, messy activity in the enrichment group – painting with pudding. This had been a favourite activity among my children when I was teaching in the US, and I'd longed to bring it to my groups in Wales, because it was such a splendid kinaesthetic experience; however, so far I had been thwarted by the simple fact 'pudding', as we knew it in America, didn't exist here. It took a fair amount of experimentation with different concoctions to find something equally easy and inexpensive. In the end, I settled on a powdered dessert called Angel Delight, which is made up with milk. It didn't have the same creamy consistency as American pudding, but it was as close as I could get and I reckoned good enough.

'Pudding painting' is essentially finger-painting with a pleasantly edible substance, and it provides an excellent sensory experience. Not only is there the actual feel of the pudding, but it's visually stimulating as well, and because it's edible, smell and taste become involved. It's also easy for little hands to manage, which is particularly important for children with special needs who often have poor motor skills. And, of course, it's fun.

I had mixed up three large ice cream tubs of chocolate Angel Delight and brought them with me, along with enough plastic aprons for everyone and a huge stack of newspapers.

It was a splendid May afternoon, all sunshine and spring-scented air, so I decided to do the pudding painting outdoors on the old playground at the back of the building rather than in the classroom. Even so, it was a messy activity, so we laid the newspapers down on the ground first, then the large sheets of finger-painting paper. I tied the plastic aprons on each child and then came through with the tubs of chocolate Angel Delight and plopped a large cup on each of their papers.

The children thought I'd lost my mind. Every single one of them. They all sat dutifully in front of their papers, incredulous looks on their little faces, and didn't move.

'Miss?' Ffion finally asked tentatively, when no one else spoke. 'Are we supposed to eat it off the ground?'

'No, no, no, no,' I said quickly and once again explained we were *finger-painting*. The pudding was meant to be our finger-paint to make a picture.

Still no one moved. I glanced pleadingly at Eloise, who was standing behind the children, in hopes of encouraging her to help them get started. Her expression was only slightly less incredulous. 'I think, like, this must be an American thing,' she said politely.

Sitting down cross-legged in front of the children, I took a sheet of finger-painting paper myself and scooped some Angel Delight onto it. I smeared it around with the flat of my hand. 'Have you done finger-painting before?' I asked the children. They each shook their head.

Lewis was the first one to try. He tentatively stuck a finger in the pudding and licked it off.

'We're using it as paint. Smear it around.' I crawled over and gently took his hand, pushing it into the pudding. He squealed, half in terror, half in delight.

'*You* try it now,' I said to Ffion, who was sitting next to him. I was counting on her, because normally Ffion was game for anything. Not this time. She shook her head.

'Come on, you guys. This is *fun*. Try it.'

Finally I looked up at Eloise, still lingering behind the children. 'Sit down next to Ffion. Get her started for me.'

Eloise hesitated.

'Here,' I said emphatically, tapping the ground as if I were directing a dog.

Eloise sat down between Lewis and Ffion.

'Have you ever finger-painted?' I asked.

Eloise shook her head.

'Well, it's very easy. You just swoosh the paint around with your hands, and in this case, the paint is pudding.'

'It looks like poo,' Eloise replied in a low voice.

That broke the ice, because, of course, once seen, you couldn't unsee it.

'Poo!' Ffion squealed delightedly and pushed her hand flat into it.

'Poo!' a couple of the others echoed.

'Look at me! I'm eating poo,' cried Bethan, and she shoved a handful of the chocolate pudding into her mouth.

And they were off. It never did become finger-painting. Instead we had a poo-squishing and poo-eating session, but the children certainly got fully into the sensory experience. There was Angel Delight smeared onto the papers, the aprons, arms and faces. I only just managed to stop Buddug from putting it in her hair.

The only child having problems was Jack. He found touching the pudding off-putting. I'm not sure he even tried it, although one of the little girls said he had stuck a finger in. All I saw was him sitting at the end of the row of children, his expression disconcerted.

Concerned that Jack would find the others' exuberant play too overwhelming, I suggested Eloise take him back inside with a small amount of pudding and paper and see if she could encourage him to experience it. I hoped this would give Eloise a chance to play with the medium as well, which I suspected she was unwilling to do in front of me.

This didn't happen. When the other children and I returned to the classroom, Eloise had Jack on her lap in the reading corner and they were doing nursery rhymes. The finger-painting paper with a glob of Angel Delight in the middle was untouched.

On the drive home, Eloise and I deconstructed the lesson. She found it hilarious that I had carefully planned a lesson and it had degenerated into 'poo-painting'. I laughed with her because it *was* funny, but also because I could tell how tickled she was that the kids had got one over on me. I agreed that the day had turned out very differently to what I'd planned, but I said I was okay with it. Poo-painting had all the same benefits as finger-painting, plus we had had a great laugh. I mentioned how fixated children that age generally are on poo and pee and other bodily excretions, so that no doubt added to the fun.

We then fell into a companionable silence that lasted several miles.

'I didn't want to touch it,' Eloise said quietly, the amusement gone from her voice.

'Yes, I noticed. But that's okay. Everyone seemed a bit unsure.'

'I didn't think of it then, when we were with the group. Other than just that I didn't want to do it. But now . . . I was just thinking . . . I was remembering . . .'

A pause drew out. Eloise continued to look out the side window. 'Can I tell you something?' she asked softly.

'Yes, of course.'

'He used chocolate sauce . . . that thick kind that you put on ice cream. He would put it on his dick. Stand in front of me and dribble this chocolate sauce along his dick. That's what this made me think of . . . He never thought of Angel Delight, but it's what it reminded me of. Of food where it shouldn't be. Having to touch his dick with the chocolate sauce on it. He wanted me to put it in my mouth.'

I didn't know who specifically Eloise was talking about. I assumed it was Darren, her mother's boyfriend, who had taken the pornographic pictures, but I didn't want to ask. I didn't want to interrupt her.

'My mum wasn't there. He never did it when she was there. He did it when she was at work. He didn't work. He took care of me. That's what he called taking care of me.'

'But it wasn't, was it?' I said. 'And it was not your fault it happened. You know that, don't you? He should never have done that.'

'Do you mind that I told you about it?' Eloise asked. 'Do you mind that I talked about, like, sucking dick?'

'No, of course not.'

'Do you believe me?'

'Is it the truth?'

'Yes.'

'Then I believe you.'

'My mum didn't. When I told her, she said I was a scummy bint for making up something so vile. I said I'm not making it up. She told me I was lying.'

'How awful for you. I'm sorry that happened.'

'I haven't thought about it in a long time. But the pudding reminded me of it. It made those thoughts come back into my head.'

chapter thirteen

A couple of peaceful weeks followed. Spring was moving into summer. The days lengthened and grew warm, and while in Wales there is never a time of year that could be described as 'dry', we had enough sunny Wednesday afternoons that we could hold most of the enrichment group's activities outside.

Eloise blossomed in this time. She was cheerful and enthusiastic when I collected her each Wednesday afternoon to drive to Pen-y-Garth. Most journeys were filled with tales of what she was doing at school. At fourteen, she was beginning to prepare for the GCSE exams. The children in her age group were currently going through teacher assessments, which would greatly impact their future. This was when decisions were made about which subjects to study and whether or not the child should take a vocational or academic route through the next few years.

Eloise was not a motivated student, to the point that I felt we were doing well just to keep her in school and not truanting. Nonetheless, she talked with unexpected enthusiasm about choosing GCSE topics. I knew she would more likely end up on a vocational course and we discussed these options as well. She was most interested in catering, because this was what one of her friends was going to do.

We had an equally smooth few weeks in the enrichment group. We took advantage of the nice weather and enjoyed a teddy bears' picnic down by the small stream that ran just beyond the playground fence. We held a treasure hunt that Eloise enjoyed more than the children – my clues proved to be a bit too difficult for this group, so she got to solve almost all of them. And we started practising for the village's eisteddfod, which was a local festival of music and poetry that mirrored the national Welsh cultural event.

Our group was assigned a well-known folk song, 'Cyfri'r Geifr', about counting goats. It's a fun song with a strong, repetitive chorus, so I felt we stood a good chance of learning it well enough that parents could be proud on the day of the eisteddfod.

It was due to be held during the last week of school in mid-July. After that came the six-week summer break, during which time our group would also take a break and not meet again until early September.

In mid-June, I picked Eloise up on a Wednesday afternoon, as usual. It was a warm day, verging on hot. She was wearing her school uniform, but her blazer was slung over her shoulder and her tie was off, leaving the top of her blouse unbuttoned. When she got into the car, she gave a gasp of relief.

'Whew, hey?' I said. 'It's hot out there today, isn't it?'

She readily agreed.

There was a long pause, then Eloise said, 'Can you see what's different?'

I looked over.

She fluffed her hair, so I knew it was that, but I couldn't see what was different about it, other than that it was loose when it was ordinarily tied back for school. Because of the natural curl, Eloise's hair always had a rumpled, almost slept-in look. Unlike most girls who skimmed their hair straight back and fastened it with a ponytail holder, Eloise usually had hers parted on the side, the front bit held out of her face with a plain hair grip, because it was so thick and unwieldy, and it was then tied back. All I ever really noticed was that it wanted a trim as the ends were very uneven, but I knew length was important to her.

'You are so unobservant,' she said, her tone affectionate and a little patronizing, when I didn't guess.

'So tell me,' I said.

'I put colour in it. Blue dye. Mostly it's washed out, but I think there's still enough to see. Can't you see it?'

I couldn't, but I mumbled something about not being able to look closely because I was behind the wheel, so safety and all that.

'I put it in on Friday night when I was going out clubbing.'

I said nothing.

'Me and Olivia both dyed our hair. She came over beforehand, so that we could do it together. She put pink in hers and I put blue. You get it in sachets at Boots, and you just wash it in. It's pretty good.'

'I'll have to have a better look at your hair when I'm not driving.'

'Olivia's got shorter hair. Just to her shoulders, so it was so much easier for her. Her hair's dark brown, so pink was good for her.' Eloise was smiling in a blissful, almost dreamy way. 'Her hair's so shiny. It's straight, you know, straight as can be, and when you touch it, it feels like silk. It really does. I so wish I had hair like that.'

I smiled. 'Yes, me too. I think us curly headed girls get a bad deal.'

'So we put the colours in our hair, and then we did our make-up. I did Olivia's for her. I'm pretty good at it. I'm thinking maybe I might be a make-up artist someday. You can be that, you know. It's a proper job. I'm thinking maybe I'll tell the careers counsellor that's what I want to do. I could work on film sets, probably.'

I smiled. 'That sounds quite exciting.'

'So I did Olivia's make-up for her, because she wanted to look extra lush. She's got this pink lipstick. I think she nicked it, to be honest, because it's L'Oréal and cost, like, £9. But it's such an awesome colour.'

Eloise continued along this vein for several more minutes, elaborating in greater and greater detail about this Friday night spent with Olivia. I was almost certain everything she was telling me was fantasy. There were no clubs in the village where Eloise's foster home was, and, while there certainly were clubs in the towns down on the coast, I couldn't imagine Eloise would be going to any. She was a fourteen-year-old who looked fourteen, and, for the most part, acted it. While she was savvy enough to get herself around the area on the buses, she didn't have the street smarts of the older kids. This tale was Eloise's idea of what you did before you went clubbing, her fantasy night out.

As she continued to elaborate on this adventure, I was trying to decide how to respond. In this instance, Olivia didn't seem to be Heddwen Powell, and I wanted to explore this, to see if I could tease this Olivia out, but how should I tackle it? I was reluctant to thwart Eloise's casual, unhindered conversation, because she so seldom talked to me like this, and I definitely didn't want to spark a power struggle over the veracity of what she was saying.

'That sounds like you had fun,' I said.

'We did. We went to this club down on the seafront called Mickey's. Do you know it?' Eloise asked.

I did know it, or at least I knew of it. It was a low, modern building with a huge, garishly coloured sign above the entrance, which I passed often because the area's only big supermarket was on the same street. The name stood out because our dog was named Mickey, so our family had a running dad joke about the club being our dog's sideline business. Every time we drove by someone in the car had to say, 'There's where Mickey earns his dog food money.'

Before I could respond to Eloise, she continued on, enthralled with her story. 'We met these lads there. They were, like, twenty and twenty-three. They wanted to take us down to the beach. Olivia said, "Oh, we better not go, because we might get in trouble." But the two lads had some cider and they said, if we came with them, we could have some too. But Olivia didn't want to. So we stayed in the club. This other bloke, he was, like, twenty-six, and he bought us a blue WKD. I call them "Blue Wickeds". Because that's what they are, if you get drunk on them!' She looked over and grinned. 'And that's what happened to poor Olivia. She got *so* drunk. She was puking. I held her hair back for her. I put my hand on her forehead and made sure she was okay. We were, like, hours in the bog until she felt better. But we were laughing about it later, because she got so sick. And it was blue puke!'

'Wow, that's an exciting story,' I said.

Eloise's eyes narrowed. 'You think it's a story, don't you? You think I'm making it up.'

I looked over.

'You think I'm a liar.' Anger frittered the tone of her voice.

'There are different kinds of true and not true. I don't think you're lying, but I do think it's a story,' I said.

Eloise made a sudden, irritated explosive noise. 'See why I don't ever tell you anything? You never believe a word I say. Nobody does. Nobody ever *hears* me.'

'I do hear you, Eloise.'

'You don't. You bloody well don't. It's like I'm not even here. It's like I'm talking into a vacuum. Everything I say, it comes out as something else. You're not hearing *me*.' And with that, she clamped her arms around herself and didn't speak for the rest of the journey.

*

I regretted having this conversation on our inward journey, because Eloise arrived at the group in a Very Bad Mood. She didn't want to get out of the car. I knew better than to let her sit there, as she would probably take off, so I made her come in with me. She plonked herself heavily into one of the small chairs as I gathered all the children together for the activity.

'What's the matter with her?' Ffion asked me.

'Eloise is feeling a bit upset,' I said.

'Don't talk about me like I'm not here,' Eloise squealed.

'*T'eisiau cwtsh?*' Ffion cried in her most motherly voice and ran over to throw her arms around Eloise.

'STOP IT!' Eloise cried and roughly pushed Ffion away.

'Yo!' I said, and gave Eloise the evil eye.

Ffion's face dragged down in a grimace of tears.

'Come here, sweetheart. Do *you* want a cuddle?' And I put my arms around her.

Our first activity was playing one of those dire therapeutic 'games', that isn't really a game at all. I always felt fraudulent describing them as such, but picking up a random card to talk about difficult subjects did seem to make it easier to discuss them.

The purpose of this game was to help the children learn different ways of self-soothing when upset. Although the activity had been planned well before I'd left home, Eloise felt that it was directed right at her, and once again she was in a huff.

As we sat down in a circle on the rug, I asked Eloise to sit on the opposite side of the circle from me in order to help the children on that side read the cards, because several weren't readers. Then I set the scene, explaining that when we feel upset, there are helpful things we can do to make ourselves feel better. The cards give examples of things to do and we would take turns drawing the cards and discussing and practising what they said.

I drew the first card to demonstrate. It said: 'Stop, Look and Listen', but showed a drawing of someone in a superhero costume. I explained that the card was encouraging me to take a moment to notice my environment in detail, because when we are upset, we often forget about everything else except feeling bad. Taking out a moment to notice the details of what our senses tell us – what we can see, what we can hear, what we can touch – helps us come back into ourselves. I pointed out that the person on the card was wearing a superhero costume, and this was telling us that, when we did this, we wanted to do it as if we had superpowers of observation. We wanted to notice details as if we could super-see, super-hear, super-touch. When we had finished that, we wanted to turn our superpowers inside and notice internal sensations. What were our muscles doing? What were our thoughts? I showed the card to the children and then described what, in that moment, I super-noticed externally and internally. Then I asked them to try it.

When it was her turn, Rhian, who was next to me, drew a card that said 'When you are feeling upset, do some stretching and relaxing exercises to let the tension out'. We all tried a few stretches and deep breathing. Thus, we continued on around the circle, reading each card and practising what it said.

It came to Buddug's turn. She drew a card that suggested

imagining how you feel as a creature. As she couldn't read, she held the card out towards the centre of the circle for someone to help her.

Eloise was nearer to her and reached over for the card. 'Pretend whatever you're feeling is an animal', she said as way of explanation.

'Tiger!' Lewis burst forth. 'That'd be me when I'm angry. *Rooowwwwrr!*'

'It's her question, not yours,' Eloise snapped. 'Come on, Buddug. Look. What animal do you feel like? Look at the card.'

I could tell by Buddug's expression that she had no idea what was going on.

'*Look at the card*,' Eloise said emphatically. 'Look. See? See, there's a dinosaur. The kind that *bites* you. That's how that kid is feeling. He feels like a dinosaur that's going to *bite* you. *Hard.*'

'El,' I said under my breath, to warn her to calm down.

Of course, by this point several of the other children had picked up the dinosaur theme and two or three small T-rexes rose from the circle, plus Bryn, who appeared to be doing a zombie impression. Buddug shrunk back, her frizzy little pigtails bobbing.

'*Look at the card*,' Eloise hissed.

Buddug burst into tears.

'Arrrrghhh!' Eloise shrieked in exasperation and threw the card down.

Eloise's grumpiness passed into ennui as the session progressed. In ordinary circumstances, her main conflict technique was avoidance – if things got too rough, she just took off. Having to stay present through her initial anger with me and then her frustration with the group left her tired and jaded. We were both relieved when the afternoon was over.

'That wasn't one of our better days, was it?' I said, as I pulled the car out of the car park.

Eloise made a puffy humph.

'How are you feeling?' I asked.

'Like I don't want to talk any *more* about any*thing*.'

Knowing this was true, it seemed better not to push it, so I desisted.

We both took refuge in the splendid scenery as the car climbed up out of the valley where the village was and reached the open countryside. I toyed with the idea of putting the radio on, as I found music deeply soothing after a difficult day, and I particularly liked music when I was driving. I preferred classical, so my car radio was always tuned to the classical station, and this to me was perfect music for the panoramic view. I knew classical wasn't Eloise's preference, but I wouldn't have minded if she wanted to change it to something more youthful.

Just as I was about to suggest this, Eloise said, 'I hate Bud-dug. She's so stupid, she drives me crackers.'

'Yes, I've noticed you have problems with her.'

'Can I tell you something?'

'Yes, of course.'

'It isn't very nice. You might not like me if I say it.'

'Go ahead.'

'I want to bully her.'

'Why do you think that is?'

'I don't know. But I think about it a lot.'

A long pause followed.

'How can somebody make you want to mistreat them, when they are not actually doing anything to you?' she asked.

'It may be more helpful to ask, "Why do I feel like mistreating someone?"'

'That's the same thing as I said.'

'Not quite. You were asking what it was that Buddug did. But it's not Buddug. The reaction is inside you. Buddug might do exactly the same thing with someone else and they wouldn't feel like bullying her. So, it's not about what she's doing. It's about what it triggers inside you. Because relationships are always two-way. Her actions, your reactions.'

'Yes, okay. So why do I feel like that? Just looking at her pisses me off.'

'Why do you think that is?'

'I don't know. That's why I'm asking you, so don't keep putting it all back on me. Because I want her to cry. That's what I feel when I see her. Like she asks for it. Then, when she cries, I feel better.'

'Sometimes people do trigger us. It's worth thinking about why, because it usually helps us understand things about ourselves. Plus, I'm glad you told me. That way I can help keep things sorted out between you, because obviously I can't let any bullying happen.'

'No, I know. I wouldn't ever do it. I was just saying.'

chapter fourteen

Olivia was still on my mind. I wanted to ask Eloise about her directly, but every time I tried I was met either with anger or silence. The relationship between Olivia and Heddwen was particularly confusing to me.

Not that Olivia wasn't a regular part of our lives these days. More and more often Eloise used at least part of the car journey to Pen-y-Garth to tell me about Olivia's most recent exploits. In the beginning I just heard the occasional one-off comment, but increasingly I was getting whole episodes.

'Olivia broke her leg. Did I tell you?'

'I'm sorry to hear that,' I replied.

'She was horse-riding,' Eloise said. 'The horse spooked and it ran away with her. It was up by the moors. Not your moors. Other ones over by the coast, you know, behind those big hills. There's a pony-trekking place up there, and Olivia goes every Saturday. Pony-trekking is one of her favourite activities. Anyway, she got to ride Lightning. That's his name. He's a proper horse, not a pony at all, not a pony. Olivia doesn't like riding ponies. She likes a horse so that she can do jumps. Lightning is a thoroughbred. A hunter, but he's owned by the pony-trekking place now. He's brown and has a white blaze on the front of his face. He's Olivia's favourite, but he isn't very well trained. He's nervous, because he was abused before. Mistreated. But Olivia has tamed him. Except he's still nervous and you've got to be a superb rider to handle him. Anyway, they were riding and he spooked at a road sign. Horses are like that sometimes. They don't understand something they haven't seen before. So he spooked at this sign and reared up and ran off from all the other ponies. Olivia had to hold on with all her might. She's an extremely excellent rider, but even she couldn't stop Lightning. Nobody could. He's a hunter, so he probably wanted to jump some fences, but there weren't any. Just rocks. And that's where Olivia fell off, right near this big rock, and when she did, her leg hit the rock and it broke.'

'Wow! That's some event,' I said.

'She's in a lot of pain. She had to go to the hospital and now she has a cast on her leg. And I've been helping her. She can't do much for herself.'

As with so much else Eloise told me about Olivia, I was certain this was fantasy. I knew, however, I wouldn't get anywhere if I challenged the veracity of the story. Eloise would get angry and shut down and that would be the end of it. It seemed better to let her talk, because then at least I knew what was occupying her thoughts, and I hoped I would get a better handle on what was going on. In her heart of hearts, I think Eloise knew that I was aware Olivia was imaginary. It made for a strange relationship when she told me these stories, but for now it seemed best just to bide my time.

One pattern I noticed emerging was Olivia's tendency to have very bad luck that usually ended with her injured or ill and needing Eloise to care for her. I tried to walk a fine line on all this. I wanted Eloise to feel validated as a person, worthy of being listened to, and I wanted her to feel she could tell me things without being judged. At the same time, I didn't want to be over-encouraging of this strange state, partway between fantasy and fakery, so when the tales got very elaborate I tended to steer us back out of them.

On this occasion, after the detailed horse-riding tale, instead of pursuing what happened next, I asked, 'What do you like best about Olivia?'

There was no immediate answer.

I had noticed this long pause on other occasions when I'd asked a direct question about Olivia, and I found it interesting, because it was as if I'd back-footed her. I wouldn't have expected to be able to do that if Olivia were a well-developed fantasy figure. Having had a vivid internal world myself, I knew I would have been able to give an instant answer to a question like that. I was so familiar with my imaginary world and the people in it that I could have answered for them as quickly as I could have for my own family. Eloise didn't seem able to do this. She would tell these long, involved stories of her activities with Olivia, but when asked directly about her she came up blank.

Previously, I'd interpreted this sudden silence as defensiveness. She didn't want to let me in on this secret part of her. She was keeping it safe and private. That had been my own reason for not speaking about my imaginary world when I was her age. Now, here, as we were driving to Pen-y-Garth, and Eloise had just told me this whole involved story of Olivia's horse-riding, it occurred to me that perhaps I'd over-interpreted Olivia in the past, that I had assumed Eloise was having the same sort of experience that I'd had as a teenager. My character Delilah had been the most important part of my internal world, and I had lavished a huge amount of time on creating her persona, on developing the minutiae that makes an individual, and, indeed, even creating Delilah's own internal mental world. Consequently, I 'knew' Delilah in as much detail as I did any of my friends. Perhaps the reason Eloise clammed up when asked these direct questions about Olivia was because Olivia wasn't such a well-developed character. Eloise stopped talking because she simply didn't have an answer. This told me that what mattered to her was her interaction with Olivia, and Olivia was less a person in her own right and more a plot device.

When Eloise didn't respond to my question, I said, 'It sounds to me like you enjoy helping Olivia. When she's poorly or hurt herself, you take care of her.'

Eloise nodded. 'But she's tough and good at stuff. And she takes risks. Not stupid risks. Risks because she's very brave. She'd take care of me in a minute, if I needed it. So when she needs me, when she gets hurt or something, I take care of her.'

'That sounds like a good arrangement.'

'Yeah . . .'

There was a subtle note in that 'yeah' that I recognized as the inflection made when a conversation has gone too far and it's time to stop. My questions had taken Eloise out of her private realm of Olivia as vulnerable superhero. My responding as if Olivia were a real person was stretching Eloise's credulity. This wasn't my imaginary game and I could hear how uncomfortable Eloise was beginning to feel with my doing it.

Good, I thought, because it indicated that Eloise recognized it as fantasy.

'Remember a few weeks ago, when we were talking about visualizing things in our minds?' I asked. 'About how they were almost real? How they were real in every way except being tangible?'

Eloise nodded. 'Yes.'

'I told you how that all came about because of an imaginary world I had in my head when I was little,' I said. 'My world was like watching TV in my head. My character Delilah was a grown-up, right from the start, right from when I was four or five, and she lived in a whole different world to mine, her own world, with its own rules.

'My family kept expecting me to outgrow it. Maybe that would have happened, except that something big occurred the year I turned twelve. For complicated reasons, I was taken away from my family and sent to live with a family I didn't know. I had to leave the parents I'd grown up with. I had to leave all my pets. I had to leave all my friends and move six hundred miles away to a place I'd never seen before. Everything I knew changed. The only thing that stayed the same was Delilah. The only thing that came with me was the world inside my head.'

Eloise's forehead puckered. 'Hold on, say what? Why did you get taken away?'

'It wasn't for bad reasons. My mother remarried. You wouldn't think that would be such a big event, but it was, because I had never lived with my mother before that. My grandparents had raised me. But the year I was twelve, she remarried, and she wanted me to go and live with her.'

Eloise's brow was still drawn down. 'So, you're saying you didn't know your own mother?'

'I knew her. But she lived over a hundred miles away from me, and I only saw her when she came to visit. I loved her dearly because she was like a fairy godmother then. She'd bring me sweets and presents and take me out places, because she had a car and my grandparents didn't. But I'd never lived with her. The only mother I'd ever known was my grandmother.'

'That's not as bad as what happened to me,' Eloise said dismissively. 'At least your mother liked you. At least you knew who you were going to live with. I never did. I just got jerked around.'

'Yes, you're right. You've had a much tougher time of it,' I said, 'but it was still challenging for me. She wasn't used to being my parent, and we didn't know each other very well. I didn't know the man she had married or his children, and it was so far away from my grandparents. That's like, if Social moved you again, they suddenly thought your next foster home ought to be in Inverness.'

'Wow, I wouldn't like that, going to Inverness,' Eloise said. 'That's not even in Wales.' She paused a moment to consider all I'd said. 'It was almost as if you were in foster care too, except that it was with people that you liked. Because that's what happens to me. I get settled someplace and then, next thing you know, I'm somewhere else with a bunch of complete strangers. *All the time.*'

'Yes. I know. It's one reason I've shared this with you. The other reason I've shared it is because that might be why I ended up keeping my imaginary world when most kids outgrow things like that. It was something of my own when everything else had been taken away. Something familiar. The rest of my life got turned on its head, but my imaginary world remained just as I left it.'

Eloise turned her head and looked out the side window. We were on the last long descent down from the hills into Pen-y-Garth.

'Now that I'm older and I look back on it, I think it was okay that I kept it,' I said. 'People get funny about imaginary stuff. They can make you feel there's something wrong with you for having people in your head that they can't experience, but I think it's okay. As long as we keep in mind that there's a difference between what's in our head and what's out here, as long as we don't expect other people to accommodate what we've created, it's fine. My imaginary world helped me survive a very difficult time in my life, and I think that's a good reason to have an imaginary world. We do what we need to do to survive.'

*

The school eisteddfod was looming. I was pleased my children had been invited to participate; I wouldn't normally have expected to be included, but this village was small and their eisteddfod equally minute, and who could resist a bunch of tinies massacring a song about goats?

The big challenge was teaching my children how to work as a group. I should have been content with simply herding them together in a bunch and getting them to sing. However, as most of them were already familiar with the words of the song, it being a popular Welsh ditty, I thought to switch it up a bit. Our boy Jack had a stunning voice. He often sang to himself under his breath, so I knew he knew all the words to the song. As the song involves a question – 'Where is the goat?' – and then a response, I thought it would be lovely if Jack sang the question, and the rest of the children sang the response, counting the goats in: 'The white goat, white, white, white' or 'black goat, black, black, black' or whatever colour goat was coming along.

How hard could this be?

Ha.

To start, I brought in a cassette recorder with the music so that everyone could sing along. I explained that Jack was going to do the first part as if it were a proper question and everyone else would answer with the coloured goats.

Jack was quite severely autistic, but he had speech, and he loved both music and repetition, so I thought we'd be okay here. I assigned Eloise the task of helping him learn his part. 'Can you sing this, Jack?' she asked, then sang, *'Oes gafr eto, oes heb ei godro? Ar y creigiau geirwon, mae'r hen afr yn crwydro.'*

Jack dutifully repeated it in his sweet, lilting voice.

'Wonderful! *Bendegedig!*' I said.

Jack repeated it again.

'Absolutely brilliant, Jack. Thank you very much.'

Jack repeated it again.

'The rest of you, quick!' I said. 'Answer Jack. Tell him about the white goat!'

And this is how it went, with Jack relentlessly singing his part and the others rushing to get in their response.

'You guys, you're fantastic,' I said, after way too much time spent singing about goats. 'We're going to blow them away at the eisteddfod. We're going to get up there and sing and we'll feel so proud of ourselves.'

'Miss? Miss, can I tell you something?' Ffion said.

'What's that, sweetie?'

'Last Christmas, during the Nativity play . . .' she paused to search for the English.

'Yes?'

'Mary puked on baby Jesus' head.'

chapter fifteen

On the ride home, Eloise was in an ebullient mood. She had enjoyed being in charge of Jack and taking part in the singing. Things had become very silly towards the end, in part because it was such a silly song, in part because we were all having fun with it. Eloise had let go of her normal adolescent reserve in a way that I hadn't seen her do before.

As we were starting up the steep lane out of the village, Eloise burst into the first chorus of the song. '*Gafr wen, wen, wen, le fin wen, fin wen, fin wen!*' and she laughed gleefully. 'It is *absolutely* going around in my head. I'm going to be singing it all night.'

I agreed it was a very sticky sort of song, and when Eloise sang another verse of the chorus I joined in. We went through the whole of the song one more time.

This tickled Eloise. Her grin was broad as she looked over. 'I'm speaking Welsh.'

'Well, yes. If you ever have a need to find where a group of colourful goats have gone, you're set up.'

This made her laugh.

A quiet interlude then. The day was beautiful, one of those peerless June days of warm sun and blue, blue sky. The mountains shimmered in a heat haze. We both remarked on how unusually close this made them look.

'This is the first time I've ever had fun speaking Welsh,' Eloise said softly. 'To be honest, I mostly skive my Welsh lessons at school.'

I nodded. 'I gathered that.'

'I'm awful at it. I think I must be one of those people who can't learn other languages, and yet they insist I take it. I don't see why. I'm a dead loss.'

'You're finding it very hard,' I said.

'My *nain* . . . she used to get so pissed off with me because I wouldn't speak it to her. I was scared to even try, because I knew she was going to yell at me for making mistakes.'

'Being yelled at for mistakes is no fun.'

She nodded. 'I could have stayed living there, if I'd been better at Welsh. I wanted to stay so much . . .'

'I think it may have been more about your dad going back to prison,' I said.

'What do they call it when you want something so badly that you end up ruining it?'

'I think the word for that is "self-sabotage",' I said gently. 'It's when we do things that get in the way of achieving what we want to.'

Eloise was silent for a moment and then shook her head. 'No, I don't mean that. I mean, like when you're a kid and you want to hold something delicate, like a bird egg, but when someone puts it into your hands, you're so afraid of dropping it that you squeeze it, and then, because you squeeze it, you break it. That's what I mean, you're trying so hard to be careful not to break something, that it actually makes you break it.'

'Do you feel that's what happened with your *nain*?'

'I don't know. Yes, I guess. I wanted to be good at speaking Welsh for her so much that I screwed it up entirely.'

'And now you feel it's your fault that you had to leave your grandmother's house.'

'I don't "feel it". I know it. Because I know that's the reason,' Eloise replied. 'She said that. She told my social worker I was too difficult.'

'That's a different reason than speaking Welsh.'

Eloise shrugged. 'It was still my fault.'

'Is it possible that instead of it's being your fault, the real issue was that your grandmother was overwhelmed? Think of it. She's an older lady, and the fact is, people don't have as much energy when they get older. She's living on a pension, so it might be hard to stretch to another mouth to feed. She has a son with addiction problems, and he keeps going in and out of prison, and she's supporting him in between times. She's got a lot on her plate. She may simply not have had the wherewithal to care for a young person.'

'But she *said* it was my fault. Because I was too difficult.'

'Blaming someone else for being difficult is often a way of disguising the fact that the problem is yours, and you can't cope.'

'But if I could have spoken Welsh . . .' Eloise said. 'But I couldn't do it. I didn't even want to try, because I knew I was going to speak wrong. I was going to make mistakes and I didn't want her to be upset with me, so I just sat there like a lump. That's what makes me difficult. I won't do things I'm supposed to, even though I want to. I can't make myself be a good person.'

With many of the children I worked with, I attended meetings as part of the team supporting the child's progress in the social welfare system. This had so far not been the case with Eloise. Because I was initially there to provide CBT and that hadn't happened, I'd lost my official status. I was now regarded as a 'befriender', a vetted volunteer who offered friendship, emotional support and guidance. I didn't miss having to attend the meetings. Sue-Pugh and I had good communications and I knew she would keep me abreast of any issues, as I would her, if anything came up on my watch.

In late June, however, there was an annual review of Eloise's case and Sue-Pugh asked if I would like to sit in and share my experiences of working with her, so for the first time I found myself around the table with the others who worked on Eloise's case. Some of the people I knew already from work with other children, and this included Meleri and Ben Stone, the Social Services child psychologist. Sue-Pugh and a supervising social worker named Jen McDonald were also there, as well as Eloise's foster parents, whom I had not previously met.

At the heart of the meeting was Eloise's stalking behaviour. We heard the very welcome news that Eloise had not been caught at the Powells' house in the last five weeks, which was a record. When Sue-Pugh announced this, there was much pleased murmuring around the table and the supervising social worker ventured a tentative, 'Have we cracked it?' Ben Stone replied probably not, although it was a promising sign that we were going in the right direction.

To be honest, I think Ben may have said stalking was still an issue largely because he had put work into a presentation on stalking, and there wouldn't have been much point in giving it if we'd already cracked it. So he ploughed ahead with a handout and Power Point, identifying those same five types of stalkers I'd read about – the rejected stalker, who arose after the breakdown of a relationship; the resentful stalker, who believed he/ she was the victim and needed to get back at the individual he/ she perceived had mistreated him/her; the predatory stalker, who was usually male, stalking females, and the stalking arose in the context of deviant sexual interests; the incompetent suitor stalker, who targeted strangers or acquaintances to get a date or otherwise short-term relationship; and the intimacy-seeking stalker, who had delusional beliefs about a relationship with the target of their attentions. Understanding the nature of Eloise's stalking behaviour was crucial, he emphasized, not only so that we could manage the behaviour but also to identify how much of a risk she was to Heddwen Powell.

Discussion arose over whether Eloise fell into the incompetent suitor category or the intimacy-seeking category. Loneliness was a factor for both these types, as well as a general inability to form 'normal' relationships, particularly with the opposite sex. The discussion wandered from here onto the topic of

Eloise's sexuality. Was she gay? Both Sue-Pugh and her foster mother said that Eloise never mentioned boys, never showed an interest in the usual early adolescent preoccupations with boy bands and male celebrities, never talked about crushes. I was asked if I'd noticed a lack of interest in this area, and I acknowledged that I had had very few conversations with her about boys. I added that I wasn't sure, however, that this was diagnostic. Some children are slower than others to become interested in these sorts of things, and this may have been simply a developmental variation, but we also had to remember Eloise's past. The sexual abuse and pornographic activity she had been exposed to in middle childhood would have had a marked impact on her sexual development, and we needed to be alert to this.

The conversation continued along this line before Ben Stone brought us back to his categories of stalkers. People more or less agreed that Eloise still fell in the original category – intimacy-seeking – and that she was imagining she had a relationship with Heddwen even though one did not exist. Ben said this was called an 'erotomanic delusion'.

I was finding the whole conversation a bit off-putting. We were not taking into consideration just how complex psycho-sexual behaviour was, and it seemed reductive to think of Eloise's relationship with Heddwen as 'delusion'. Erotomania is when a person, typically female, believes another person, usually more powerful or of higher social status, is in love with them. I felt Eloise was indeed seeking intimacy, but I continued to think it was not necessarily sexual. There are so many other kinds of intimacy – familial, maternal, friendship – and there was the caretaking aspect that she showed in her relationship with Olivia. It was at this point I brought up Olivia.

When I mentioned this, talking about how Eloise portrayed herself as strong and nurturing in her conversation about Olivia, I started to realize that no one else in the meeting, including Eloise's foster parents, was aware of Olivia. *What?* I was shocked to discover this. Olivia and the confusion between Olivia and Heddwen had been such a big part of my conversations with Eloise from the very first meeting. It was hard to conceive of the possibility that others didn't know. Had Eloise genuinely never said anything to Sue-Pugh or Meleri? To her foster parents? Once I mentioned it, Meleri thought she recalled Eloise saying something about an Olivia once or twice when she was first moved from the Powells', but Meleri had not taken any special notice. She only vaguely remembered the comments now and couldn't bring the context back to mind.

So I told them what I knew. I talked about how, in our early meetings, when Eloise talked about Olivia, she seemed to be meaning Heddwen Powell. I mentioned that whenever I asked her directly why she was calling Heddwen by this other name or if Heddwen and Olivia were the same person, Eloise had always demurred. So there had been some confusion in the early days about who Olivia was, but latterly the two had seemed to separate out. Eloise now told me stories about Olivia that I knew were entirely unrelated to Heddwen.

I said that recently I had noticed an interesting pattern to the Olivia stories. Increasingly, whenever Eloise talked spontaneously to me about Olivia, she put herself in the care-taker role. This intrigued me, because Olivia had originally seemed to be a typical fantasy superhero who was strong and beautiful, and able to do all the things that Eloise couldn't. Now, however, she was often ill or injured and required Eloise to take on the role of strength. I said I hoped this shift might indicate that Eloise was seeing herself more often as competent and powerful.

The others listened closely as I spoke, but when I finished there was silence. No one said anything. I looked around the table. Finally Jen McDonald nodded. 'That's very interesting.'

There were other nods. Then Ben Stone said, 'I think every-thing we see fits with the intimacy-seeker stalking model. Here we've got a lonely, socially inept girl who wants a relationship with this older girl, who is popular and successful. Who's to say it's not rooted in sexuality? If she has lesbian tendencies, this may be a crush that's gone too far.'

Disappointed, I said, 'I think this Olivia thing is worth unpick-ing. It may be worth looking at in its own right rather than as part of the stalking model.'

'If only we had time,' Sue-Pugh said, a complex note to her voice that was both empathetic and perhaps a little patronizing.

And then they moved on. The discussion turned to Eloise's education, to her tendency to truant, to what would be the best track for her through the exam maze that formed children's last few years in secondary school. I realized that was it. Nothing more was going to be done. I'd thrown all that information out and, yes, it was interesting, but that was all. Move along. Nothing to see here.

The National Eisteddfod of Wales is held in August. It is a hugely popular annual arts and music festival celebrating Welsh culture and language with origins that stretch clear back into the ancient era of the Welsh bards. At its heart is a series of competitions, mostly in music and poetry, which conclude by 'chairing' a national bard, who is, in essence, a Welsh-language poet laureate, and the prize is literally a chair. This practice harks back to ancient times when chairs signified high status. Kings and princes sat, while the rest of the populace stood or squatted on stools. Latterly in Celtic courts, the bard – the musician and poet of the court – was given a chair at the nobles' high table, in recognition of the importance of the arts in Celtic culture.

Our little local eisteddfod did its best to bring the pomp and ceremony of the National Eisteddfod to the village school. Garlands of flowers bedecked the playground behind the new school building where the eisteddfod was being held. A marquee had been set up, because we all knew not to trust the Welsh weather, and within was the small stage and rows and rows of chairs for the children and the spectating parents.

There were six other groups of children performing before us, which meant Eloise and I had the task of keeping eight little bums on seats for the better part of thirty minutes.

The first 'Miss, I need a wee,' came literally five minutes into the programme. The announcer had not even finished the introduction.

This was Bethan asking, so I nodded towards Eloise. 'Can you take her?'

By the time she returned, Jack was getting antsy. He was not 100 per cent reliable regarding the toilet, and as he had a star role I didn't want him to appear on stage with wet trousers. 'Can you take him?'

Ffion was next. 'Miss, I really have to go.'

'Just take them all,' I muttered to Eloise when she returned with Jack.

'I *took* them. Right before we came in. Everybody went,' she hissed back, interpreting my frustration as accusation.

'Take them again.' And so off trooped the other six.

They were gone more than fifteen minutes, at which point I was getting nervous because we were due on stage after the next group recited their poem. I kept glancing towards the marquee flap, hoping to see familiar little faces appear. Could I trust Eloise to keep track of the time? Did she even have a watch? I looked at Jack and Bethan and wondered if they could do the goat song as a duet.

All that worry for nothing. In trooped my group with five minutes to spare.

Ffion sat down next to me. 'Miss, I need to tell you something.'

'Can it wait, Ffion? Because we're just about to go on stage.'

She pursed her lips and shook her head. I could tell she was bursting to say something. 'Eloise *wedi brathu* Buddug.'

'I'm sorry, what's that?'

'Eloise *ei ddannedd i mewn i* Buddug!'

The marquee was noisy and I just wasn't able to make out what she was saying. I could hear the frustration in her voice, but whatever she was telling me was, in that moment, just a step too far for my Welsh. Raucous applause all around us didn't help. I didn't understand what she said, but I pretended I did. Putting on a sympathetic expression, I touched her face lovingly and said, 'I'm sorry to hear that.' Then our group was called. All the children stood up and paraded onto the stage.

It was, of course, as adorable as you would imagine. Jack sang his part perfectly, his lilting voice rising up above the murmur of the crowd. The others replied with off-key gusto, counting in the variously coloured goats. Most of the audience was singing along by the last verse.

The day was a typical midsummer's day, warm and sunny, with just enough humidity to make it heavy. Large bumblebees bobbed along a flower border just beyond the schoolyard wall, their buzzing magnified by the heavy air. The tables of refreshments had been set up in the shade of the school building, because the marquee was becoming too stuffy.

When all the performances were finished we were ready to move out to make our choices from the spectacular array of cakes and biscuits laid out on the tables. Eloise left on toilet duty again while I took the others out to find their family members and get plates. I had Buddug with me, as she was the most inclined to wander off, and I had not yet seen her mother. As I leaned down to ask her which piece of cake she wanted from the table, I noticed an angry-looking mark on her arm. 'What's happened here?'

Buddug shrank back from me.

I held her arm up and looked more closely to see very clear teeth marks. Remembering that Ffion had tried to tell me something just as we were ready to go on stage, I looked around the schoolyard for her. Seeing her with her two older sisters, I beckoned her over.

'Do you know what happened here?' I asked her and showed Buddug's arm.

'I told you!' Ffion said emphatically. 'Eloise *wedi brathu* on her arm.' She made a clicking noise with her teeth. When I hesitated, she bit her own arm. '*Wedi brathu!*'

'Eloise *bit* Buddug?' I asked.

'Yes,' Ffion said, 'in the toilets. Because Buddug didn't hurry up.'

Shocked, I examined Buddug's arm more closely. It wasn't immediately obvious that it was a bite mark, but it was angry and red and the skin had been broken in one place.

'Buddug didn't hurry and Eloise *cydiodd* her arm. Buddug started to cry and Eloise *yn crac*,' Ffion said.

I lifted my head to scan the yard for Eloise.

'Miss? Miss?' Ffion said, tugging on my arm.

I looked down at her.

'It isn't the first time. *Mae hi'n pinsio.*' Ffion pinched her own arm to make sure I understood.

'She's pinching Buddug?'

Ffion nodded.

'Has she hurt anyone else? Or just Buddug?' I asked.

'She pinched me too,' Ffion said with a downcast expression, 'because I was slow.'

My heart sank. 'Okay, thanks for telling me. That was the right thing to do.'

chapter sixteen

I waited out the additional forty-five minutes or so until the festivities had finished, because there was no point in ruining the other children's time or causing a scene. In the interim, I ensured Eloise was no longer alone with any of the children, and I sought out Buddug's mother to explain that there had been an incident and Buddug had a minor injury because of it, and, of course, to apologize profusely. Then I sat, distracted and upset, waiting to deal with Eloise.

When the children had all finally left with their families, Eloise and I returned to the classroom in the old school to pick up our belongings. Once inside, I closed the classroom door and told her to sit down. Alarm immediately sharpened her features.

I explained that I had seen Buddug's injury and wanted to hear what had happened.

'Buddug bit herself,' Eloise said. 'She's that stupid. She was upset because I wouldn't let her go back out to you until she'd had a wee. She was being horribly slow and just faffing about, so I tried to get her to hurry up. She started crying and wanted to go back out, but she didn't even have her clothes done up. So I said no and held her back. She had a paddy and that's when she bit herself! I didn't tell you, because it was just then that they had to go on stage and do their song.'

'Ffion said that you bit her.'

'Me? Why the fuck would Ffion say that? She wasn't even in the stall with us. Why the fuck would *I* bite Buddug?'

'Ffion said you became impatient with Buddug because she was being slow.'

'Ffion was cross with me because I made her stop farting around with the water. And I got cross back, because she was into *everybody's* business. I couldn't do anything in there without Ffion butting in, so I was sharp with her. But I didn't *bite* anyone, for fuck's sake. I'm not six.'

'Did you pinch her?'

'Ffion? No. Of course not. I've never touched any of them. I never have. Never. Ever. You know that. You've never seen me do anything like that, have you? Ever. *Ever.*'

'I need the absolute truth here, because this is quite a serious allegation. I saw Buddug's bite mark and it seems odd to me that she'd bite herself that hard. She's never bitten herself before.'

'That might be true, but it doesn't mean I did it. Why would Ffion say that?'

'I do understand how frustrating the kids can be,' I said. 'Buddug, in particular, can be trying. I understand impatience. It happens. Sometimes we act out in ways we shouldn't when we feel frustrated.'

'I. Didn't. Do. It.'

'And I remember your saying that Buddug got on your nerves, that she brought out angry feelings . . .'

'*Once*. I told you once I didn't like Buddug, and now that's all you're going to remember, isn't it? Shit, I wish I never told you anything.'

'This is very important, because we're working with little kids here. We're entrusted with their welfare. I can understand frustration. Sometimes things happen. But I need to know. I just want your side of it, Eloise.'

'There *is* no "my side of it". How many times do I have to say? *I didn't do anything*. Read my lips. I. Didn't. Do. It.'

'I want to believe you. However, Ffion said there have been other times when you've pinched children because you were angry with how slow they were,' I said.

'What is it with that little fuckwit? Why is she saying these things about me? She's horrid. She's just stirring things up. You know that. You know she gets in everyone's business.'

I sat back and regarded her.

'I wish I'd never come here,' she muttered. 'I never wanted this. You made me do this, come here with these little retards and do your work for you. And this is what I get for it. Well, fuck you. That's all I'm going to say.'

I could tell Eloise was very close to running away from me, and I didn't want that, so I didn't respond. Rising from my chair, I gathered the last of my things together.

'Come on,' I said. 'Let's go.'

'I'm not getting in a car, just so that you can yell at me for the next half an hour. I'll walk home.'

'I'm not going to yell at you. Come on.'

'No. I'll walk home,' she replied.

'That's not an option.'

'I'll get a bus then.'

'That's not an option.'

'*Why?*'

'Because it's not an option. Come on.'

There was a long moment's stand-off, with Eloise at the table, me in front of the door so that she could not escape.

Giving one last huge, annoyed sigh, Eloise finally rose to her feet and followed me out.

The atmosphere in the car was ripe. I stuck to my word and didn't say anything further; my mind, however, was going full throttle ahead, because what now? This was very much the end of Eloise's visits to Pen-y-Garth. It would be a serious breach of trust to let her back with the children until this was completely sorted out. As it was, I'd have to report it both to my charity supervisor and to Sue-Pugh.

I sighed. I wanted to believe Eloise's version of this, that somehow Buddug had managed to bite her own arm so badly it had left broken skin, that Ffion was imagining she'd seen Eloise do it, that there had been no pinching. But Buddug had no history of tantrums or self-harming behaviour in the time she'd been with me, and why would six-year-old Ffion make all this up? The cold hard fact was that I'd entrusted these young children to an adolescent with known mental health issues, and that was how it would be seen.

So what now for Eloise and me? Was this going to be the end of our time together? It felt like it. I couldn't imagine how the various authorities would allow us to continue.

The drive with its mountain vistas and winding small lanes lush with summer wildflowers proved calming. I didn't see this beauty when we first left the village, so caught up was I in the drama, but slowly my thoughts began to settle. Eloise's anger also dissipated. Her breathing softened. She turned her head to watch the scenery.

'Do you hate me now?' she asked quietly, about twenty minutes into the ride.

'No, I don't hate you. But I'm sad this happened.'

'So am I,' she said softly.

'Can you tell me why it happened?' I asked.

'I don't know.' She sighed. 'I'm just stupid, that's all. I ruin everything I touch.'

The hardest conversation was with Lynn, my supervisor at the charity. She'd taken a chance on letting me do this with Eloise. It was something I'd sensed was already outside her comfort zone, but she had been willing to trust my judgement. Now I had to admit my judgement had been off, that this difficult, disturbed girl needed more supervision than I'd given and here was the result. I knew all the children's parents would need to be formally notified and then each child individually interviewed to find out the extent of what had happened. Pinching, biting. Anything else? Anything worse? We needed to ascertain that. This wasn't a task for me alone. Lynn wanted two senior members of the charity to accompany me through the interviews.

Would I be allowed to resume the enrichment group? I was suddenly discerning that I, as well as Eloise, was about to be removed. It was the end of the school year, Lynn replied, and things were at a natural end. She'd make the decision after the summer break.

And then the hardest question. I looked across the desk at Lynn. She was a small woman, much smaller and more delicate than I. Her features were sharp, almost rat-like, except that her hairstyle softened them, leaving just a sense of shrewdness, or maybe that was the directness of her gaze. 'What of Eloise?' I asked. 'May I continue working with her?'

'We'll see,' she said.

The other difficult conversation was with Sue-Pugh. 'That girl,' she muttered when I told her, and she didn't continue the thought.

I acknowledged that the fault was mine. I had thought it was all right to give a nearly fifteen-year-old the kinds of responsibilities I had, but clearly I was mistaken. I felt sad about this, because what had we come to that everyone had to be supervised all the time?

'Are we going to discover anything worse?' Sue-Pugh asked and I knew that unsaid in her question was whether or not Eloise's abusive behaviour had extended to sexual misconduct.

I shook my head. 'I don't think so. I honestly don't. My sense is that she just lost patience and acted out.'

'Are you sure? This girl will have seen more willies in her short life than you and I combined. And she was the same age as those children in the group when it was all happening to her. So maybe five-year-olds turn her on.'

'It was a bite on the arm,' I said. Nothing I'd seen supported sexual misconduct.

'Biting is a twisted thing to do at her age. There had better not be something worse that she's hiding.'

I sighed, because I had no way of proving Eloise's innocence on this front. Or guilt. 'She gets frustrated easily,' I said, 'and she doesn't seem to have good control when she's upset, but nothing, *nothing* made me think she would be abusive. She's been upset with me on other occasions when we've been in the group, and nothing ever came of it.'

I didn't want to minimize what Eloise had done. It was unambiguously wrong, and the biting was pretty icky, but I did feel the behaviour was the result of normal emotions inappropriately expressed, rather than some sociopathic tendency. I'd been with her enough to get a sense of that sort of thing, I said, and then pointed out how easy it was to make what had happened sound worse than it was, that how the more we dissected it, the more frightening it sounded.

Sue-Pugh shook her head. 'She's had a lot of chances, that girl, and she's not very good at taking advantage of them. She could be living with her father and grandmother, but she failed that. She could have kept her act together at the Powells' and still be there, but she failed that. She could have completed the CBT that was offered and changed her behaviour, but she failed that. She could have knuckled down at school, because she isn't stupid, but she's failed that. And she's had you working with her for what? Almost a year now? How many kids in the system get a chance like that? And here she is, as much of a mess as ever. Blowing it one more time.'

I knew Sue-Pugh didn't mean this in the cold-blooded way that it sounded. This was her own frustration talking, because what could you do with an underfunded, overstretched social care system and kids who, for whatever reason, were unable to grasp the few opportunities that came their way? Why *hadn't* Eloise done more to help herself? There were countless reasons – neglect, rejection and sexual exploitation among them – and that was without taking into account that she was a teenager, and who among us had their shit together at fourteen? I understood Sue-Pugh's feelings but I also understood Eloise's.

The two days that followed were spent in Pen-y-Garth, talking individually with each of the children in my enrichment group, and then with their parents. Accompanying me through all the meetings were Gillian Hughes and Bill McClure from our charity.

Talking to the children was a challenging experience because most of them had not witnessed what was going on between Eloise and Buddug, and those who had gave confused versions. Buddug had had a tantrum. Eloise manhandled her out of a toilet stall. Ffion was dancing around, being Ffion. Everyone was in agreement about those things, but then it started to vary. According to Bethan, Eloise was holding Buddug but her real anger was directed towards Ffion, who kept interfering, and at one point she flicked Ffion on the head to get her to move away. Ffion told us Eloise had got very angry with Buddug, and when she tried to help, Eloise pinched her. She then went into an elaborate story about Eloise pinching her other times too, whenever she thought Ffion was being slow.

Mercifully, there was no evidence of sexual misconduct. While everything in question had happened in the toilets, the children were in agreement that Eloise had not intruded on any of them while they were using the toilet or while they were undressed. Even so, I felt awful listening to all this. I remembered Eloise telling me about her urge to bully Buddug, how she had felt antipathy towards the little girl from the very first meeting. I had noted it, because it had seemed odd to me that she would take such an instant dislike towards someone; and I'd turned the thought over more than a few times, wondering if it was related to Eloise's earlier life, but I hadn't believed that she would act on it. I now felt horrible. Should I have seen this coming? Should I have had the foresight to take preventative measures? If so, what ones? Never let Eloise out of my sight? Talk to her ahead of time about appropriate ways to deal with her frustration? With children who dawdled in the washroom? Yes, possibly, to all of those things.

Most of the parents seemed unconcerned. Indeed, Bethan's mother already knew about the incident, because Bethan had told her that Eloise had flicked Ffion on the head with her finger. 'I asked her why,' Bethan's mother said, 'and she said because

Ffion was being awkward and trying to get all the attention on herself, so I told her, well then, Ffion won't do that next time, will she?'

Then came Buddug's mother. We met her in her home, a small, terraced council house at the end of the village. Buddug's mother greeted us at the door, a baby on her hip, and two children younger than Buddug hanging on to her. Buddug stood in the background, looking confused.

We entered a small, cluttered sitting room heated by an open coal fire, despite its being July. Damp clothes hung everywhere. Even with the fire, the room was cool, dank and smelled of urine. Buddug's mother greeted us politely but I sensed an underlying suspicion. She offered us tea and apologized for having no biscuits.

The interview was conducted in Welsh, so Bill did it all because my Welsh wasn't fluent enough. Indeed, I couldn't follow much of it, and found my attention wandering. I watched Buddug, who remained apart from us. She had a plastic teapot and small cup, and I think she was trying to imitate us with our tea, but she wasn't really managing. She was just sitting, holding the toys and looking over at us.

I smiled at her. She gave a quick quirk of her lips in response and looked down. Her two younger siblings surrounded her, took the teapot, squabbled noisily over getting the cup as well, and she surrendered them. Then Bill called her over so that we could all look at her arm. The bite mark was no longer noticeable.

The conversation went on. The two younger siblings squabbled more loudly. The baby began to cry. The coal fire burped and a puff of smoke wafted across the room. Buddug's mother cursed it, shouted at the two children, jiggled the baby and smiled apologetically at us. She said something about 'Never mind'. I felt sad without quite knowing why.

And that was it. The investigation was over.

Lynn was satisfied that nothing more sinister had been going on. She said that she was no longer comfortable having Eloise attend the enrichment group, but as far as she was concerned I could resume the group after the summer break. I left her office relieved but saddened for what had been lost.

I think we made the matter into a bigger deal than it was. In times gone by we would have handled it with a stern talking-to and then moved on, but in these days emphasis was on the victim and the victim's psychological welfare. While, on the one hand, this was exactly as it should be, on the other hand, such concern gave an unbalanced picture of what had actually happened. While in no way did I condone what Eloise had done, I felt her behaviour was a reflection of her own difficult circumstances and should have been treated more as a teaching opportunity to help her than to punish her. Reacting too harshly was likely to cause only resentment or dejection, not behavioural change. I was sorry for this, because at the end of the day she was a victim too.

Once the investigation had been completed and the dust was settling, I went to see Eloise. She had recently had her fifteenth birthday, so I picked her up from her foster home and took her for tea and cake at a nearby tea shop.

To clear the air, I brought the case up as soon as we sat down. I summarized what had happened as I didn't want to dredge up all the gory details. I talked about Lynn and the people from my charity and how we'd gone out to see the children. Then I explained briefly what the kids had said and how the report had gone and what the conclusion was. Everything was now resolved, I said, so we'd put it behind us.

Eloise's attention seemed to be mainly on the pot of tea. She kept taking the lid off and peering into it, as we waited for it to brew. Putting a spoon in, she gave a tentative stir, then lifted the teabag out and peered in again to see how strong it was. A second pot of hot water was always provided with orders of tea at this shop, so that what continued to steep after the first cup could be diluted. Eloise plopped the teabag into this second pot, which isn't how it's normally done.

'Do you want to pour it?' I said, feeling a little frustrated, because it wasn't at all apparent if she'd been paying any attention to what I'd said.

Eloise pulled the cups over, poured the tea, and pushed my cup across towards me. She took the lid off the pot of hot water, fished the tea bag out, put it back in the original pot and then added the hot water to it.

'Are you quite finished?' I asked.

'Yeah,' she said distractedly.

'So . . .' I said, 'the matter is sorted at Pen-y-Garth.'

'Oh good, my cake.' Eloise had ordered a piece of Victoria

sponge to go with her tea and it arrived at the table. She tucked into it enthusiastically.

Realizing I wasn't going to get a response over Pen-y-Garth, I asked, 'How's it been going with you?'

'Okay.'

'What's been happening?'

'School's finished.'

She reached over and poured herself a second cup of tea. For the first time she looked up and met my eyes. 'You want more tea?'

'No, thanks. I'm good.'

She turned her attention back to her food. 'Olivia's been sick,' she said. 'She had to go to hospital. They think it's her appendix.'

I sat back.

Eloise nodded as if I'd responded. 'Yes, it started two weeks ago. She had a lot of pain, here, on her side.'

'How have *you* felt?' I asked. 'Have you been okay?'

Eloise's eyebrow rose up in a querying expression. 'Yes, of course I have. Why would you ask that? It's Olivia I'm talking about. She's been awfully poorly. She could have died, if no one had realized. Appendixes can be that way. They grumble on and then they explode inside you and you can die. Olivia's appendix exploded. She nearly died.'

chapter seventeen

My charity took a break at the same time as the local schools were out for the summer, because most of us volunteers had young children of our own to look after. Added to this was the whole matter of summer holidays, of people being gone for a fortnight here and there. In the end, the charity found it easier to pause work for those weeks and resume in the autumn.

I was reluctant to break with Eloise at this point because it had taken so long to form any sort of rapport with her. Everything between us felt 'almost'. We'd almost had a workable relationship. We'd almost untangled Olivia as an imaginary character. We'd almost sorted out the stalking with Heddwen, or at least we'd almost got around to talking about it. These things had begun to feel to me like goals that could be reached. Then we'd had the bad knock over the incident at Pen-y-Garth. So it didn't feel like the right time to stop work. Unfortunately, I had no format in which to continue. Consequently, when I dropped her off after our tea at the cafe, I said goodbye knowing it was goodbye for six weeks.

Traditionally I took my daughter home to Montana during

the summer break. This gave my mother the opportunity to enjoy being a grandmother, and my daughter a chance to connect with her Montana heritage. It also gave us the guarantee of proper summer weather in which to enjoy our activities, something that was often in short supply in Wales.

For this particular summer we were gone the entire six weeks. School started for my daughter on the fifth of September and we didn't arrive home until the third. My husband had stayed in Wales over the holidays because of his work, but also because his father was at an age where we didn't want to leave him alone on the farm for so long. There was a joyful reunion at the airport when my daughter and I returned, happy but exhausted.

The drive home took almost two hours and during this time my husband brought us up to date on various family matters. My father-in-law had had several small health scares regarding skin cancer. His much-loved dog had been ill with asthma, which had upset him much more than his own health had, and my husband complained about what a trial administering asthma medication to a dog had been. Our elderly cat had died, something my husband had kept from us while we were abroad, and I wished he'd kept it a little longer, as our overtired young daughter found the news very distressing.

'Oh yes,' my husband said, 'and someone named Pugh kept phoning.'

I asked if any message had been left and he said no, just that she had phoned several times and didn't seem to understand that I was away for the entire summer.

When had she first phoned? I asked. Right after I'd left, he replied.

As with the cat's demise, I wished he'd kept this news for after I'd got home, had a shower and some sleep, and possibly moved my head a little closer to the Welsh time zone. However, hearing that Sue-Pugh had phoned on several different occasions, I knew I had to contact her as soon as possible.

'She went over to the Powells'. This was literally twenty-four hours after you'd last seen her. She didn't say it had anything to do with you, but she did say something about Pen-y-Garth. But I get ahead of myself,' Sue-Pugh said. 'She went over to the Powells'. They were away for the weekend, so no one was home. Eloise broke into the house. Then she got up to serious mischief. She slept in the beds. She took food from the cupboards. She got into Heddwen's make-up and clothes. Worst, she defecated on the floor of Heddwen's bedroom before she left.'

'Wow,' I said under my breath.

'Understandably, this was the last straw for the Powells. They contacted the police, not us,' Sue-Pugh said. 'There was a massive palaver. To make matters worse, Eloise didn't return to her foster home after her time at the Powells', so no one knew where to find her. We looked in all her usual haunts, everywhere she goes when she's skiving school. *Nada*. It was *ten days* before the police tracked her down. So I'm afraid we didn't have much choice about what to do with her. She's gone to Cae Newydd.'

My heart sank. Cae Newydd was a secure children's facility

on the far side of the county. While I appreciated why this action had been taken, it was bad news for Eloise.

'I tried to contact you,' Sue-Pugh said. 'Eloise kept saying it was over what had happened with the Pen-y-Garth group, and how everything went wrong, how you were cross with her and she was going to kill herself. She was going to do that at the Powells', but then she didn't, but then she wished she had, and . . . oh, crikey, such a mess. She kept talking about how she thought she'd been doing so well, but then it had all gone to hell. I tried to tell her I was sure she was reading you wrong and you weren't angry with her, but she's not willing to listen. She's been on suicide watch ever since she got to Cae Newydd. So, I was hoping once you were back and settled you could perhaps spend some time with her. I think it would mean a lot.'

From the kerbside, Cae Newydd looked like a school to me. A modern building from the 1970s or 80s, low and flat-roofed, it had an entrance into a central hub area and then three spoke-like arms radiating out. The fence around the property, however, left no doubt about what kind of facility it was.

At the door I was met by a tall, pale man named Iain, who identified himself as the day manager. There was none of the casual friendliness of most of the group homes I had worked in. Iain gave me a visitor's pass on a lanyard and politely introduced me to other staff as we passed down a corridor to another building hub that hadn't been visible from the street. Here there was a large, communal day room. Furniture delineated different areas: sofas and chairs around a television in one section, a pool table in another, a glass-enclosed staff area with chairs along the back wall. In the section nearest the staff area there was an assortment of beanbag chairs, pillows and large, poufy loungers. It was here Eloise was waiting for me.

'Hiya,' I said as I came over.

She smiled self-consciously and murmured hello.

'I brought you some chocolate.' I took a large Dairy Milk bar from my handbag.

Her eyes lit up. 'Thanks!'

Then silence as we both waited for staff to go back to what they were doing before I arrived.

My intention was to break the ice by talking a little bit about my time in Montana, nothing too exciting so she'd not feel jealous of my daughter or bad for being locked in a facility while I was swanning about in the sun, but just enough to get us comfortable talking to each other again. However, I sensed immediately that this wasn't a good idea, that any kind of reference to families and activities on the outside would hurt her.

'I like your hair,' I said. 'Have you cut it?'

She nodded. 'A little.'

'It looks nice.'

She nodded.

'So tell me how things are going?'

Eloise shrugged.

'Sue-Pugh phoned me about what happened. I wasn't able to respond at the time, because I was seeing my family in America. I only just got back on Thursday. But Sue-Pugh has filled me in.'

'She's not my social worker any more. I'm with Mrs Thomas again.'

'Yes, I heard that, and I'm pleased,' I said. 'I know Mrs Thomas well.'

'I like her better,' Eloise said. 'She's got good clothes. Sue-Pugh looks like she climbed out of a charity dumpster.'

'Sue-Pugh's nice, though,' I said.

Eloise grimaced. 'To you, maybe. But then she won't have fucked up your life.'

'She's fucked up yours?'

Eloise shrugged.

'In what way?'

'She put me in here, for one thing.'

I watched her.

Eloise pursed her lips. 'You're going to tell me I fucked my own life up, aren't you?'

'No,' I said. 'I was going to ask you your side of things.'

Eloise shrugged.

'Sue-Pugh filled me in, but it would be great if you could tell me what happened.'

Again Eloise shrugged.

'I would genuinely like to hear what you have to say about things.'

No response.

'I know you've probably had to go over this a million times with other people. And probably you don't want to talk about it,' I said, 'but it would be helpful for me to hear.'

She opened the chocolate bar and broke the first row into

small squares. She offered me one and as she did, she met my eyes. Her expression was hard to read. It didn't have the surliness that her body posture implied. Instead, there was almost a longing in her eyes, as if she were hoping I would do or say something, but it wasn't clear to me what.

I accepted the chocolate from her, and for a few moments we disguised the silence by eating.

'So, how's that girl doing?' Eloise asked.

'Which girl?'

'Betty.'

This caught me off guard. 'Betty who?'

'I mean Buddug. Is her arm better?'

'I haven't seen her since school broke up, but when I last saw her, yes, her arm was better.'

'I was dreaming about her last night. Isn't that weird?' Eloise said. 'I mean, all the things that I could be dreaming about but I wake up with her on my mind. Maybe I knew you were coming. Maybe I sensed it and that's why I dreamt of her.'

'Maybe,' I said.

'I was thinking about her red hair. I mean, man, that girl's hair is *red*. She's going to get teased so bad when she gets older. Especially since it's so curly. What would you ever do with hair like that to make it look good? And I hate to say it about her, but she was thick. She was that kind of thick that doesn't get better, you know? The kind of girl that stands around on the edge of the playing field, watching everyone else, because she's too thick to figure out what's going on in time to join in.'

'You were thinking about all the things that are going wrong for Buddug.'

Eloise brought a hand up and studied her fingernails. 'They don't let you have nail clippers in here,' she murmured.

'You told me one time that Buddug reminded you of your sister.'

'That was a lie. I don't know why I told you that. Evie didn't have red hair. Doesn't have red hair. I assume she's still alive, so I shouldn't talk about her in the past tense. She doesn't have red hair. Her hair is brown, like mine. Just ordinary hair. I'm not sure why I said to you that she was like Betty.'

'Buddug.'

'Yes, well, whatever.'

'That was an unexpected thing to lie about,' I said.

'Are you cross?' Eloise asked.

'No. It's of no consequence. I was just wondering why it happened. Because it *was* of no consequence. I didn't know your sister. Why did you want to tell me that Buddug reminded you of her?'

'I dunno. It was a long time ago that I said it. I don't know what I was thinking.'

I regarded her.

Eloise broke off another row of the chocolate.

I remained silent.

'I dunno. I sometimes just say things. They come out of my mouth without passing through my brain first,' Eloise said. 'I mean, I hardly ever think of my sister. To be honest, I don't even remember what she looks like. If I ran into her on the street, I probably wouldn't know it was her.'

'But on just that occasion, you thought she looked like Buddug.'

'I guess. I guess it's maybe because you paid a lot of attention to Buddug. I used to be jealous of my sister. I was always kind of jealous,' Eloise said softly. She shrugged. 'I mean, why did she get adopted and I didn't? Why did I have to go back to my mum? My life could have been different.'

'And Buddug reminded you of her . . . ?'

'I wanted my sister to be like that, stupid and ugly and out of chances, but she's not. The truth is, whenever I looked at Betty, I'd see me.'

'Buddug.'

'Buddug, Betty. It doesn't matter. Nobody will ever remember her name. She's just one more invisible girl.'

chapter eighteen

'Will you come again?' Eloise asked.

I'd been sitting with her on the beanbag chairs for the better part of two hours. Beyond her, I could see the desk area where staff were gathering. They were waiting for me to leave. No one had yet come over to say time was up, but I was aware of them glancing at us with increasing frequency.

'I don't have anybody,' she said. 'Lots of the kids here, they've got, like, mums or dads who come to visit them, but I don't have anyone. So would you come again?'

'I'll have to see,' I said.

'I mean, if you don't *want* to . . .'

'No, that's not what I'm saying. I need authorization. I'm not a relative, so I can't just turn up, even if I'd really like to,' I said.

Eloise made a face. 'Don't bother.'

'It's not a bother. I just need to clear it, that's all.'

She flopped back wearily on the beanbag. 'Just fuck off. It doesn't matter.'

'That's not what I said.'

'This place feels like prison. Basically it is. For kids. A kids' prison. I mean, what's the point? I don't know how long I'll have to stay in here. I've nothing to look forward to.'

'I'm sorry it feels like there's no way out.'

'There isn't.' She looked at me briefly. 'Well, there is. I could end it. That's what I feel like doing. Cutting myself here and here,' she indicated her wrists. 'That's what this other kid did. Just last week and it sounds good, that feeling of everything running out of me.' She looked over at me. 'Does that bother you? That I talk like that? That I say I'm going to kill myself?'

'I don't want you to do it, if that's what you're asking, because it's not a solution,' I said.

'I don't see why it isn't. Otherwise I'm going to rot in here till I age out, and then what? I'll be homeless, because I don't have anywhere to go. I mean, what am I going to do when I don't even have this place? My mum has no idea I'm in here. My dad has no idea I'm in here. And if they did, they wouldn't give a shit anyway. They've got their own messed-up lives to deal with. And the system sure doesn't give a shit. So I might as well save everybody the trouble. Save the government the trouble. They're the only ones that know I'm here.'

'I'm very sorry you're feeling so rough,' I said. 'But let's not take quite such a long-term view. You've got three years before you age out. That's well in the future. Let's keep the focus right here, now.'

Eloise shrugged. 'Why? You just said you're not coming either, so why do you care how I think?'

'I didn't say I wouldn't come. I said I need authorization.'

'Same thing.'

'No, it's not the same thing, Eloise. And what you're thinking about isn't a solution. I know that in the heat of the moment it feels like it would be, but it's not. So, please, don't hurt yourself. There are better things we can try, and I'm happy to help you with them.'

She grew tearful as I spoke.

Opening my handbag, I took out a tissue and handed it to her. 'Remember when we first started?' I asked. 'I was trying to get you to do some exercises? About how our thoughts and feelings and behaviour are all interconnected?'

With the back of her hand, Eloise wiped away her tears. 'I'm sorry I'm crying,' she whimpered.

'It's okay. Totally okay.'

'I know you want to go, though. I'm sorry for making you stay.'

'Sweetheart, don't worry about it. You're not making me stay. I'm here because I want to be. If Iain thinks it's time for me to go, he'll come over and tell me. Or if he wants you for something else, he'll come over. Until then, we're good. We're okay.'

Silence flowed in around us as Eloise struggled with her composure. I looked beyond her to the staff desk, because I knew it was likely Iain would come over soon. Catching his eye, I shook my head very slightly in hopes he would understand to give me a few minutes longer.

'Do you remember when we first started?' I asked again. 'And the things we were trying to do then?'

'Yes,' Eloise said.

'Would you be willing to try some of these things now?

Because if we did it that way, I'm sure I'd get the authorization to come again.'

Eloise regarded me doubtfully. 'What would I have to do?'

'I've been trying to think of which things would be most helpful. When Sue-Pugh told me about all this and I knew I'd be coming out to see you, I started considering what we could do together here at Cae Newydd. The thing I think you might enjoy most is a journal.'

I went on to explain in detail how a journal could be used therapeutically, and what sorts of things she could write about. I kept the ideas very general, so that they would feel doable; to write about what her mood was at that moment, what her feelings were, and anything else she wanted to add – dreams, incidents, fears, difficulties.

'But I don't have a journal.'

'No, I know. I'll bring you one. I'll find an especially nice one for you and bring it with me next week when I come.'

Back again to my charity and my supervisor Lynn, who made jocular remarks about my tenacity. We discussed various approaches. She wanted me to return to the CBT format, and thus followed a lengthy discussion about whether or not a fifteen-year-old would be mature enough to do cognitive behavioural therapy via a journal. My sense was that this would be too abstract an approach for Eloise, but journaling itself was a valuable skill. I told Lynn about how, when I was teaching, I had had good experiences even with very young children using journals, so I felt Eloise could cope with this. She needed a safe space in which to express herself, particularly given her suicidal thoughts, and as I would be going over the journal with her, it would be a space where she was heard. Lynn held tight to the idea that it should follow a prescribed format. She wasn't comfortable with open-ended journaling, so we compromised. I would ask Eloise to answer a set of loosely CBT-based questions as the basis for her journal entries.

Feeling buoyed by this positive step forward, I went to the local bookstore to find an attractive journal. I remembered how, in my own adolescence, having the right materials had been such an important part of writing for me. I recalled spending ages trawling through stationery shops, looking for notebooks with covers that were the right colour or had an appealing picture on the front, and then sizing up various pencils and pens for how they fitted my hand or coped with my left-handed grip. Those were happy memories. Eloise did not have the freedom to indulge her individuality in this way, so I wanted to do what I could to make the notebook feel distinctive and personal.

When I arrived the next week, I was escorted to the beanbag corner again, where Eloise was waiting. I now realized this was our work space. It wasn't ideal, as the large room was in the hub of the building, and there was a lot of to-ing and fro-ing of other people in the background. They didn't bother us, however. Most were in transit from one of the long corridors to another or doing things around the staff station. No one was intentionally noisy, but I occasionally found it difficult to focus, so I'm sure Eloise did as well. Also it was not very private, which may have been part of the reason for placing me there. These were increasingly litigious times.

The journal I'd chosen had a purple cover with a drawing of hummingbirds among flowers and the words 'Dream and Imagine' rather tweely inscribed across the top in silver letters. It was pretty and not at all like the standard-issue exercise notebooks given out for writing at school.

Eloise turned it over in her hand, first one way and then the other. The cover was corrugated with fine ridges and she ran her fingernail across them, making a noise. She did it again. 'You could play this as an instrument,' she said, and did it several more times in a rhythmic fashion.

Notebook-as-musical-instrument had not been my intention in getting her this particular notebook, but I said nothing.

Eloise turned it over again and ran her fingernail over the ridges on the back. Then she touched the area where the picture of the hummingbirds was. 'That's flat,' she said, and looked up at me.

I had the sense she was trying to get a rise out of me. This made me wonder if she was perhaps expecting me to take it away from her. Perhaps this itself was a type of self-sabotage, that rather than risk the hurt of caring about something and having it taken away, she would reject it herself in a way that made me take it.

When I didn't respond, Eloise finally opened the journal and looked at the pages. 'Look, it's got lines on all the pages. This isn't any different from an ordinary exercise book, except it's got a spiral.'

'The spiral makes it easier to write in, because you can open it out flat.'

'What am I supposed to write?'

'Good thing you asked,' I said cheerfully, and whipped another sheet of paper out of my satchel. 'Because here's how we're going to do it.

'Each day, I want you to write about an event. What's an event? I hear you ask. That's something that's happened to you that's given you strong feelings. Say, for example, you are watching a television programme. You are sitting there, minding your own business, enjoying what's on the telly, and suddenly someone comes over, picks up the remote and changes the channel. That's an event, because it starts a chain of feelings. So, I want you to write down what the event is. What happened? Next, tell me what your feelings are. What feelings did the event evoke? For instance, someone taking the remote and changing the channel while you were enjoying a telly programme would make you feel how?'

Eloise shrugged.

'A bit angry, huh?' I asked. 'Annoyed? That's how I'd feel.'

'I guess.'

'The next thing, what did you do in response? Someone has taken the remote. How do you respond?'

'I dunno.'

'If it were me, I might say, "Please change it back. I was watching that."'

'Or you could smack 'em,' Eloise added with a wry smile.

'Well, yes, that's another reaction. So that's the third thing.

197

Four is your response. Did you plan what you did or did it just happen? That's the fourth question. And the last one, what was the outcome?'

Eloise rolled her eyes. 'I'm never going to remember all that.'

'Not to worry, because I've made up a little cheat sheet for you to keep in the notebook to help you remember.'

'I'm not going to be able to do that. It's too much writing.'

'I'm sure it won't be, once you get the hang of it. Let's try it now. Let's talk through an example. Start with the event. What's something that's made you feel strong emotions lately?'

Eloise shrugged.

I leaned back on my beanbag and watched her.

Eloise shrugged again.

I noticed how much she'd grown recently. She was losing some of her puppy fat. Her limbs had lengthened. The leggings she had on were too short for her.

Eloise put her hand over her eyes. 'Man,' she said in an overwhelmed tone, as if I'd just asked her for recitation of the Magna Carta. I couldn't help but smile.

'Pissed off. I feel pissed off right now. I don't want to be in here. I don't want to be doing this. Why can't I have a normal life, like everyone else?'

'Good. So there's your event: right now. And there's your emotion: pissed off.'

'"Right now" is not an event,' she countered. 'It's a time.'

I ignored her. Reaching out, I took the journal from her hands. Uncapping the pen, I wrote 'Right now' and then 'pissed off' on the first page.

'*Hey!*' Eloise cried. 'I thought that journal was for me, not you. Why are you writing in it?'

I handed it back to her. 'You can do the writing then. So we have the first two – the event and the emotion it provoked. Do you remember what comes next? It's "How did you respond?"'

'Well, the event is bloody well being in here. Having to do stupid stuff.'

I gave her a long look.

'Not that this is stupid,' she added quickly, albeit with a bit of sulkiness in her voice, 'but *this*.' She swept her arm out. 'Because I wouldn't have to be doing this,' she pointed to the notebook, 'if I didn't have to cope with *this*.' Another broad sweep of her arm.

'Can we refine that into something we could write down?' I asked.

'No.'

I gave her another long look.

'I'm feeling pissed off because my life is shite. Because that's the event. I'm in this shithole place.'

'Okay,' I said. 'If you don't want me to write that down, then please write it yourself.' I held out the pen.

A heavy sigh. Eloise took the notebook from me and wrote 'Shithole' and then 'very pissed off'. She crossed that out and wrote 'Ultra mega pissed off'.

'So, that's one and two. Third thing to write down: what did you do? What was your response to being pissed off in this shithole?'

'Wrote it down in a bloody book.' As she said that, she grinned and then laughed.

I laughed too. The ice was broken.

'This is ridiculous, you know that, don't you?' she said.

'Yes. A lot of life is.'

Eloise laughed again. 'Question four: "Is that what you planned?"' she asked. 'Or did it just happen?' Before I could answer, she wrote, 'Life just happened to be ridiculous' and said, 'Question five: What was the outcome of that?' She looked over at me.

I smiled.

'So?' she said. 'What's the answer to that?'

'I think we've wandered off the track here,' I replied. 'The questions don't really make sense any more.'

Eloise grinned. 'Well, there's your answer. Life is ridiculous. And nothing makes sense. That sounds pretty right to me.'

chapter nineteen

The rest of my visit with Eloise was pleasant. She continued to be unenthusiastic about the structure I had tried to impose on the journal, but she complied good-humouredly, showing that she understood the steps, even if every one of them was 'stupid'.

I suspect much of Eloise's resistance came from low self-esteem. I think she found it hard to accept the gift of the journal, that her strong sense of worthlessness, of being nothing more than a bit of society's flotsam and jetsam, made it difficult for her to see my behaviour as sincere. Perhaps this was why she only ever seemed comfortable when she was doing something unambiguously useful, such as making tea.

Because of this, I was careful not to ally my coming to see her too closely with her doing the notebook. That would make it easy for Eloise to sabotage herself and 'prove' she was a hopeless failure, who could never change, so I tried to keep it to a firm but light-hearted, 'This is what we'll do together'. The truth is, I did believe that these exercises would genuinely help if she could bring herself to engage with them. Even if she didn't manage it, however, it still provided a format which would allow me to come see her.

The next week rolled around, and there was Eloise, waiting on the beanbags.

'So, how did we do?' I asked after greetings were over and we'd got ourselves comfortable amidst the cushions. I looked around for the journal and didn't see it.

'Why do you always say "we" when you want to know how I did? Why don't you say "how did you do?"'

'It's just a mannerism,' I said. '"We" sounds a little more inclusive to me, because we are doing this together. It's not just you. I'm part of what's going on here too.'

'It makes you sound daft. Nobody else talks that way. I think you should just talk for yourself and not me too.'

'Very well,' I said, and smiled, 'so how did *you* do then?'

'With what?' Eloise said blankly.

'The *journal*,' I said in frustration. 'How did you get on with the journal? And where is it?'

'In my room.'

I wasn't sure if she was being passive aggressive or just forgetful, but Eloise seemed to have retained none of the reasoning behind why I was there or my connection to the journal. I sent her to get it.

She returned and flopped back down on her beanbag. I took the journal and opened it.

Day One
I had Weetabix for breakfast. And toast. And raspberry jam.
And tea. And orange juice.

I had toad in the hole for lunch. And tea. And salad. And
yogurt.

I had shepherd's pie for tea. And tea. And chips. And ice
cream for pudding.

Day Two
I had Weetabix for breakfast. And toast. And raspberry jam.
And tea. And orange juice.

And so it went.

I looked over. 'This isn't quite what we talked about doing last week.' I turned to the front of the journal and took out the folded piece of paper on which I'd written out the five steps. Opening it up, I lay it on my knee. 'One: event. Two: emotions. Three: what was your response? Four: is that what you intended to do or did it just happen? Five: what was the outcome?'

'That's what I've done. These are not wrong,' Eloise said. Her tone was nonchalant, unengaged. Pointing to the first day, she said, 'One: breakfast. Two: I was hungry. Three: Ate my breakfast. Four: Yes. Five: I was full. So I did what you asked. I just wrote it down this way, because you said I could write anything extra I wanted, so I thought you'd like to know what I had.'

I leaned back. Had she understood the assignment but decided to be obstructive? Or had she not understood it and this was the best she could manage? I was quite certain it was the former. She'd understood what I'd wanted, and she then resisted doing it as intended. Both Meleri and Sue-Pugh had told me previously that this had been an issue at different times with Eloise's schoolwork. She gave the impression of under-standing the material but then seemed to go out of her way to avoid doing it as it was supposed to be done. Was she being pur-posely oppositional? Were we back in the territory of low self-worth and self-sabotage? Was there an undiagnosed learning problem? Was Eloise genuinely unable to follow the directions and she tried to disguise it with misbehaviour? Or was she just being awkward for the hell of it? Who knew.

I re-explained what was supposed to happen with the jour-nal. Eloise's expression was one of extreme ennui. She leaned back in the beanbag and stared at the ceiling.

'Do you understand what I've asked you to do?'

'Yeah.' She dangled one leg. 'And that's what I did.'

'Not quite. We're trying to work with the feelings that get you into trouble,' I said. 'And those feelings weren't about what you had for tea.'

She shrugged and kept looking at the ceiling.

'Let's get really honest here,' I said. 'You're in Cae Newydd for a specific reason – because you broke into the Powells' house. I know that you have complicated feelings regarding Heddwen, and these feelings made you do the things that have got you into trouble. My role is to help you with that.'

'Yes, I know,' she said acidly, her head still back. 'I know it's not because you *want* to be here. You didn't have to say it so bluntly. I know nobody is here for me because they *want* to be.'

'That's not what I said. I am here because I want to be,' I replied. 'I've chosen to be here. But I'm only *allowed* to be here because we are working on the things that got you into trouble. And I don't want to lose this opportunity. If you choose not to do this journal with me, then I may not be allowed to keep coming.'

'That's just your excuse.'

I didn't want to get drawn into this particular battle, so I didn't respond. Instead, I turned to a new page in the journal. 'So, one, the event: we are sitting here, talking about issues. Two: what are you feeling right now?'

'Pissed off. You always make me pissed off.'

'Okay,' I said, and wrote that down. 'Three, what are you doing in response?'

'Nothing. Sitting here. Like a hot turd.'

'I'm hearing words, angry words. That's the response I'm hearing.'

'*Nothing*. There's nothing happening except I'm pissed off,' she replied, her voice tight. 'I feel pissed off with everything. If you want to know my response, it's about a millionth of an inch away from throwing something, because that's what I feel. Because I'm just that angry. I'm angry with everybody. But with you most of all, because you keep making me do this stupid, stupid thing.'

'Yes,' I said, 'I can hear from your voice how cross you are. So are you responding the way you intend? Or is it just happening?'

'AHHH!' she cried out loudly and rose up. The sudden noise made heads turn at the staff station. 'I don't *want* to do this!'

'Yes, I can tell,' I said.

One more squawk, then a heavy sigh and she flopped back on the beanbag.

There was a long pause, and then I said, 'Shall we try a relaxation exercise? Take a break from the journal and do some relaxation?'

'Are you going to do it? Because there you go again, saying "we".'

'Yes, I think I will. So let's start by bringing our attention into our body. Notice it. Notice how the muscles are feeling. Is there a place where it's tight and tense? I can feel my jaw clenched. Right here.' I ran my fingers under my jaw bone. 'Quite often people tighten up muscles in different places when they have strong emotions. Can you notice any of these places? Your jaw? Your temples? Your shoulders? Can you notice the muscles in those places?'

'They're fine,' she muttered.

'Okay, how about the muscles in your abdomen? Around your tummy? That's another area we tighten up.'

'They're *fine*.'

'Notice your breath. Is it smooth and deep? Is it fast? Is it short?'

'Everything. Is. Fine.'

'Are you feeling relaxed?'

'I hate this,' Eloise said.

'Can you feel your heart beating?'

'*No!*' she screamed. 'Holy Jesus, why are you doing this to me?'

There was a long pause. Finally, I dropped my shoulders. 'Okay, I give up,' I said. 'We'll stop.'

Eloise pulled herself into a sitting position on the beanbag. She kept her head down.

'When I came a fortnight ago, you were eager for me to visit you again. When I came last week with the journal, you were interested in trying it. Today, you do not want to do anything. Can you tell me why?'

'Because it's stupid. Nobody else here has to do anything like this, and I don't want to.'

'You haven't tried it, Eloise.'

'I *have*. Right there.' She swept her arm across and knocked the journal to the floor.

'You haven't tried it, Eloise.'

She began to cry. 'Please don't make me.'

I looked over, surprised. 'What do you mean?'

'Please don't make me do that, what you were just doing, where I've got to look inside my body.'

'You mean the relaxation exercise?' I asked.

She nodded. 'Michael makes us do it in group too and I *hate* it.'

'What feels hateful about it to you?'

'I don't want to look at my body. I'm ugly.'

'I'm sorry you feel that way, but that isn't quite what we're doing. We aren't judging our bodies. We were just noticing what the muscles were doing. This is helpful, because when feelings start to build, like they did during our earlier conversation, the muscles in our bodies reflect that and tense up. This can make us feel unwell physically, but it can also add to feelings of anxiety or depression. So learning to recognize this, learning how to relax your muscles when you notice them going tense, will help you feel better.'

'I know, but . . .' She was still crying. Rising from her beanbag, she went across the room to a small table in the television viewing area. She picked up a box of tissues and brought them back with her. Pulling a couple of them out, she sat down again and dried her face.

We sat a few minutes in silence, before she looked over, or rather, she turned her head in my direction, but her eyes were still down. 'Can I tell you something?'

'Yes, of course.'

'It's why I don't want to look inside my body.'

I nodded.

'But it's dirty. I don't like to talk about it, because it makes me feel dirty.'

'It's okay, kiddo.'

'When I was little, Darren used to put his willy in,' she murmured.

'Your mother's boyfriend?' I asked.

She nodded. 'He always wanted to put it inside me. I hated him doing it, because it hurt so much. Once he put it in my bumhole and it touched all my insides and made me cry so bad. But my mum wouldn't stop him. I told her what he was doing, but she said, "Don't be so disgusting." She said only dirty bints talked about doing that kind of thing, and I didn't want to be a dirty bint, did I? But I thought I was going to die, because it hurt so much. But I didn't. I kept staying alive, no matter what.'

'I'm very sorry you experienced that, but I'm glad you've told me. It helps me understand.'

'So, please don't ask me to look inside my body. Because it's like I have a scar in there,' she said. 'I know I don't really. That's what the doctor said, because they took pictures of my body. There was, like, nothing ripped. But I know there's a scar in there anyway, because I can still feel the hurt.'

This information exhausted Eloise, leaving her wrung out across the beanbag. I suggested we see if we could get a cup of tea. The children were not allowed to make one for themselves, but when I asked, a staff member at the station was happy to do it for us.

Returning to our beanbags, I considered how to use the remaining time, because it didn't feel right to return to the journal, and I now knew not to do relaxation exercises. So I said, 'Tell me what you dreamt about last night.'

This request caught Eloise by surprise. She tipped her head and looked at me with a curious expression. After a few moments' contemplation, she said, 'It was proper weird. I dreamt I was in a big house, but I didn't know the house. It was old, like a tower house – you know, one of those medieval fortress places. We visited one once on a school field trip. Only someone was living in this one. It was done up nice with furniture and pictures on the walls, and I remember walking from room to room. I didn't feel lost, but I didn't know where I was going. I was just exploring.'

She paused a moment.

'It had, like, four different floors. You know how tower houses are, like townhouses with a couple of rooms on each floor, only I'm scared to death of the stairs in tower houses. They're like those ones at Caernarvon Castle, where they curl around and around and you have to hang on to a rope for a handrail. I always think I'm going to fall to my death.

'Anyway, this tower house was like that, with the spiral stone steps, and I'd go to one floor and see, like, a sitting room, but then there were more stairs. So I'd go up those. I was so scared I was going to slip because the stairs were wet, like they always are in old ruined castles. I kept thinking I'd seen everything in the house, but then the next thing I knew, there was another staircase and another floor with more rooms. So I kept going. I kind of felt scared and lost at the same time, but I still wanted to see what was on the next floor.

'I got to the very top floor and you will never guess who was there. Prince Charles!' Eloise laughed. 'Isn't that weird? I mean, he's an old geezer, isn't he? Why would I want to dream about him? But there he was in this lovely room. And there was a table with tea and all these lovely cakes. It was a proper afternoon tea like you see in posh hotels. He said I could have some and he gave me a cup of tea. He was right nice about it, like he was expecting me, or at least he was happy to have me. So I took a cake too. Then he said, "Come, see out the window." And we looked out the window together. We were right at the very top of the building, and below us there was a forest of pine trees. I remember looking down on the tops of the trees. In the distance, there was a lake. And Prince Charles was showing it to me, like he was proud of it all.'

'What an interesting dream,' I said.

'It was a good dream. I felt nice when I woke up.'

'Sometimes dreams reflect what's going on in our waking lives, but they're in a kind of code. A tower house, for example, is a defensive building. It's strong and safe, when you are inside it.'

Eloise nodded.

'When we are going from room to room in our dreams, sometimes it can represent going from idea to idea. Especially when it feels interesting. Exploring new and different rooms is like exploring new and different possibilities. And even though the stairs were scary to you, you wanted to keep exploring. Maybe your waking mind is ready to explore new ideas . . .'

'Wow,' Eloise said. 'I didn't know you were able to do dream interpretation. You're actually way more interesting than you let on most of the time.'

I grinned.

'So what about Prince Charles?' Eloise asked. 'What did he represent?'

'I'm not sure my dream interpretation skills extend that far,' I replied.

'I think he represents a nice man. Because that's what a prince is, isn't it? Prince Charming.' She wrinkled her nose.

'Except I've never pictured Prince Charming quite that old.' Laughter followed.

'Could be.'

Eloise pondered a moment. 'I think it's reminding me there are nice men in the world,' she said. 'I do know they're not all like Darren.'

chapter twenty

Eloise was waiting for me the next week.

'Hiya,' I said, and set down my satchel.

'Look. I got us a cup of tea. Iain said I could make it.' She had the mugs set on the floor beside her. 'I did yours in this mug because it has a cat on it and I know you like cats.'

'That's very thoughtful. Thank you.' I settled into the bean-bag and accepted the mug from her.

Going through my mind was the thought: *How many times have we been here before?* Eloise, cheerful over tea-making; me, dreading the change of mood that would accompany my asking her to do whatever it was that she was supposed to be doing with me. I sipped my tea, prolonging our camaraderie for just a moment.

'I like your hair,' Eloise said.

'Thank you. It's nice to hear a compliment, because I'm feel-ing a bit fed up with it. The humidity makes it go very curly and uncontrollable.'

'You should grow it long, like me,' she said. 'Then when you get fed up with it, you can tie it back.' She tipped her head to let her ponytail fall forward.

There was a pause to sip tea.

'When I get out of here, I want to have a different style. I might get it cut very short and see if it will go curly instead of wavy, like this,' Eloise said.

'Have you heard when you're leaving here?' I asked.

'Mrs Thomas came to see me at the end of last week, and she said I might be able to go back to a foster home by winter term. She wants me to stay in her district so that I'll be at the same school for my exams.'

'That's good news,' I said. 'Are there stipulations?'

'What's that mean?'

'Are there things you have to do in order to get out?'

Eloise shrugged. 'Not get in trouble here. And I haven't. I've been earning my pass privileges every weekend. I got to go to bowling on Saturday. So that's good, hey?'

'Yes, that is good. I'm proud of you.' I paused. 'So what about the Powells?'

'What about them?' Eloise asked.

'I assume part of the deal with getting out of here involves your not going to the Powells' again.'

'Why would I go there?' she asked, as if I'd suggested Antarctica.

'*Because* . . .' I nailed her with a look. I shouldn't have needed to spell it out.

Eloise shrugged.

Putting out my hand towards her journal, I said, 'Let's have a look.'

Eloise didn't respond for a moment or two. Instead, she took another sip of her tea. Then a long sigh. Finally she gave it to me.

Day One
I am feeling very sick. It makes my body feel wretched. I am going to be sick. I puked. I puked three times. I want to feel better.

Day Two
I am still sick. I am not getting better. I have bad pains in my side and it might be appendicitis. I puked three more times.

Day Three
I am still sick. I am worse now. I am getting so sick that I might die if no one takes me to the hospital, but they can't go. It's probably appendicitis and when it ruptures I will die from peritonitis. I puked some more.

I looked over at Eloise. 'Is this an account of this last week?' I asked sceptically.

'I got better.'

I regarded her. 'This actually happened?'

'I got better.'

'Eloise, come on. This is a story.'

She didn't answer.

I repressed a sigh, because, honestly, how many ways could

this girl find to avoid doing what she was asked? 'You wanted to write a story in your journal instead of doing our exercise?' I said.

'It's not a story.'

'It's not true. This is all about someone suffering appendicitis and here you are before me, just fine. And don't tell me you got better, because no one who was that ill three or four days ago would be sitting here, happy as Larry, now.'

She drew her shoulders up in a shrug but then held them there a long moment, only letting them fall slowly. She averted her eyes.

'So suppose you tell me what this is?'

'I don't know.'

I regarded her. Her bravado was melting away. Arms wrapped around herself, Eloise shrank away from me.

'I'm not cross with you,' I said. 'I do feel a bit frustrated that we can't make faster progress with the journal, but I'm not angry. I know these things happen. So let's explore this.'

'I don't know why I wrote it like that,' she replied.

'I can tell it's a story. What were you feeling at the time?'

'I don't know.'

'I understand stories,' I said, and smiled. 'That's what I do for a living, remember? So I understand how fun they are to write. I also understand how they sometimes slip out.'

'I don't know.'

I leaned back in my beanbag. Eloise had drawn up almost into a fetal position. Her knees were up, her arms were together in front of her, her hands, one clasping the other, were pressed against her lips. I took a deep breath to release my own tension and relaxed into the silence between us.

A minute passed, two minutes, I lost track after that. Waiting quietly, I listened. At first I was listening for Eloise's breath as a way of monitoring how anxious she was, but I couldn't hear it, so I listened instead to the rather noisy silence of the large room where other people were coming and going about their business, all well distant from us.

'It was Olivia,' Eloise murmured at last.

'And?'

'Olivia had appendicitis,' she said.

'So this is a record of Olivia's week?' I asked.

She nodded.

'I remember Olivia having appendicitis once before,' I said very quietly, being careful to keep any sense of accusation from my voice.

'It wasn't appendicitis this time.'

'I see.'

'She was just very poorly.'

'We haven't heard from Olivia for a while,' I commented.

'She's better. She's still feeling poorly but she's going to be all right.' Eloise lifted her eyes to meet mine for the first time since we'd started discussing the journal. Her expression implored me not to continue.

'It's all right, sweetie. I don't mind that this happened. But can we talk about it a little bit?'

Eloise grew tearful.

'Is talking about Olivia upsetting to you?'

She shook her head, but the tears remained.

'Can you tell me, how do you experience Olivia?'

'What do you mean?' she asked.

'When you wrote this in the journal, did you imagine Olivia in your mind, and then wrote a story about what you thought she was doing? Or did it feel like you, yourself, were Olivia, and she was doing the writing?'

'I don't know.'

'Sweetie, it's all right. I'm not cross that this happened. These things do happen. But since it has, let's work with it. I'd like to know more about Olivia. I'm genuinely interested.'

'You think I'm mental.'

'No, I don't,' I said. 'I understand what it's like having some-one like Olivia. Remember that one time in the car, when we were going out to Pen-y-Garth, and we had that discussion about imaginary people? I told you I had a whole imaginary world in my head when I was your age. And yes, I remember that some people thought I was mental for it. Some people even told me so. But here I am, today, completely fine, hey? It's not crazy. It's creativity. Maybe just a bit excessive, but just creativ-ity. That's what it was for me. I was creative, and didn't quite know how to handle it, because there was a *lot* of creativity and it spilled out everywhere. So it took me a while to learn how to control it. And it's the same with you.'

Head down, Eloise wiped a tear from the corner of her eye.

'Shall I tell you what I did once?' I said. 'I was about sixteen and I found a place where you could order pencils with your name inscribed on them. So I spent all my money ordering pencils with the names of my imaginary people on them. I did it because I wanted something tangible, something that I could touch, that I could see with my eyes. I felt so wonderful every time I used those pencils, because having these people's names on the pencils made it seem as if I were touching something of theirs. It made them feel closer than just my imagination. But you know what happened? My mum found them. She tried to get me to explain them, and when I couldn't she took them off me and told me there was something the matter with me that I would do this.'

Eloise lifted her head to look at me. 'So what happened? Did you get the pencils back?'

'No. She kept them because she thought what I was doing was a bit mental and she didn't want to encourage it. I don't know what she did with them.'

'That wasn't fair.'

'I didn't think so either. I still don't think so, because I understand better now what I was doing – trying to make those imaginary people more real – and I don't believe there was anything wrong with it. But my mum was scared of it because it was different to her.'

Eloise nodded in a heartfelt way.

'So I'm thinking that's maybe what happened here,' I said, 'that you were trying to make Olivia feel more real by writing in the journal from her perspective.'

'I don't know.'

'Have people got angry with you in the past about Olivia?'

'Yes.'

'I have the feeling that Olivia might have quite a lot to do with what's going on in your life right now,' I said. 'She's turned up quite a few times over the months we've been together, you and me, but we keep ignoring her. So let's make today about Olivia. She wrote in the journal, so that tells me that Olivia wanted to be here today.'

'No,' Eloise said, alarmed. 'I was just being silly.'

'Let's just start easy. Describe Olivia to me.'

'I don't want to talk about this.'

'I recall you telling me she had brown hair. How long is it?'

Eloise appeared to be on the verge of tears again, so I smiled. Leaning forward, I touched her knee reassuringly. 'It really is all right to have this conversation. I don't think you're mental. I don't think you're bad. I don't think there is anything wrong. This is okay.'

A long hesitation and then Eloise said, 'Her hair is about this length.' She measured just past her shoulders. 'It's very straight. And it's smooth and silky brown. And she's got brown eyes and sort of light brown skin. Like she had a very good tan, only it's natural. She doesn't have to go in the sun.'

'How old is Olivia?' I asked.

'Twenty-five.'

'So she's an adult?'

Eloise nodded.

'Does she look like Heddwen Powell?'

'But my Olivia's *not* her,' Eloise said quickly. 'Olivia's *like* her, but I said that that one time, just so you would know what she looked like. I'm not just making up stories. That's what little children do, acting out superheroes and stuff. I'm *not* like that. She's not Heddwen Powell. She's *Olivia*. I'm not mental. Don't make me sound like I am.'

Eloise was becoming agitated, so I changed gear. 'If I say "Imagine Olivia" can you get a clear picture of her in your mind right now?'

Eloise nodded.

'If I said "Imagine Sue-Pugh" can you get a clear picture of her in your mind?'

'Yes.'

'If I said "Imagine Sue-Pugh drinking a cup of coffee" can you see her doing that?'

'Yes.'

'Is it the same with Olivia? Can you get an equally clear picture in your mind of her drinking a cup of coffee?'

'She doesn't drink coffee.'

I grinned. 'All right. Well, then, can you see her drinking a cup of coffee and making a face, saying "Ewww! That's awful!"?'

Eloise laughed in spite of herself, and that eased the residual tension. 'Yes, I can.'

'Is that how you usually see Olivia? From your own perspective, seeing her doing things?'

'How else could I see her?'

'You could be inside Olivia and see things from her perspective.'

This caused Eloise to pause and consider. Her brow furrowed in concentration before she said, 'I've never thought of this before. It's peculiar, thinking about how you think. But I just see her, like she's in front of me.'

'When do you first remember seeing Olivia?'

Bringing a fingernail up, Eloise chewed it thoughtfully. 'A long time ago. I don't remember exactly.'

'Did you have her with you when you were living with your dad and grandma?'

Eloise nodded.

'What about earlier? Did you have her when you were living with your mum and Darren?'

'Yes . . .' She was silent a long moment and then said, 'When I was very little, I had an imagination about unicorns. I used to pretend I was in this field of unicorns and I could ride them over the rainbow. That was before Olivia . . . I was super little, like, maybe four or something. I'd get the brush off the back step and ride it around . . . Olivia wasn't there then. It was My Little Pony. That's where I got the unicorns from.'

'What's the very first time you remember Olivia?'

Eloise again fell silent for several moments, her expression turned inward. 'I was by myself. I think it was after I got took from my mum, so I might have been . . . seven? Or eight? Olivia was there. I remember her clothes. She was wearing a navy blue shirt with rolled up sleeves. And she had a brown gilet made of leather. I don't remember what she said or did. Just her being there.'

There was a long pause. Eloise looked over at me. 'I think I'm done talking about her now. It makes me uncomfortable.'

'Okay.'

'I'm sorry about the journal. I wasn't trying to be awkward. It's just that's what was . . . I mean, you said to write down what was happening to me, and *that* was what was happening. Olivia had took over my mind.'

chapter twenty-one

Meleri and I met for lunch at a small country pub on one of the back roads that led pretty much nowhere except to other back roads. The pub had pretensions to be a gastronomic hotspot, but it was so out of the way that no one except the locals managed to find it.

The year was turning. It was one of those peerless days that Wales can have in mid-autumn when the sky is such a vibrant, cloudless blue that it looks almost enamelled beyond the gold foliage. It seemed a pity to be inside in such fine weather, but the pub had no outdoor seating, so Meleri and I chose a small table next to the window.

I had come away from the conversation about Olivia not certain what to make of it and wanted Meleri's input. To me, it seemed there was a strong possibility that Eloise was simply a floridly imaginative child and it had leaked over into everyday life, much as my own imagination had done at the same age; but knowing her traumatic past I was aware there were darker possibilities, among them dissociative disorders.

These occur when a person disconnects with the here and

now. Dissociation itself is a completely normal mental phenomenon, that allows us to separate parts of ourselves from the present, and it is something we all do many times a day. Daydreaming or being lost in thought are both examples of normal dissociation. For example, when driving a car, we may miss an exit because we are deep in thought, thinking about our job or our relationship or what we want for dinner. Our body is physically present in the car, but we have no awareness of passing the exit we wanted because our thoughts are somewhere else entirely. In this kind of normal dissociation, we snap back immediately into ourselves the moment it's required. Hence, despite being lost in thought, if a child darts out into the road we are back in the present so instantaneously that we can put the brakes on in time. Dissociation is also used to protect ourselves from stress and pain, to block out upsetting memories and to survive dangerous situations. A moderate amount of dissociation allows us to cope with difficult experiences without being overwhelmed, and in this respect it can be a useful coping mechanism. It can, however, become pathological, wherein we are no longer able to return to the present moment by choice. This is known as a dissociative disorder.

The classic dissociative disorder, known in earlier times as multiple personality disorder, now called dissociative identity disorder, is when an individual develops two or more distinct dissociated identities or 'personalities' that happen involuntarily and which may be perceived as being different ages or genders, each with his or her own agenda.

Dissociative disorders have a strong correlation with trau-

matic childhood experiences, in particular prolonged or exten-
sive abuse. The child dissociates as a way of surviving situations
that are otherwise too distressing to bear. Knowing how harrowing Eloise's early life was, I was concerned that Olivia might
possibly be a second personality rather than just excessive creativity, so I wanted Meleri's opinion.

Meleri was intrigued when I told her of my conversation
with Eloise. She said Eloise had never spoken of Olivia with her,
but then paused and corrected herself. She had, indeed, heard
Olivia mentioned, but at the time it hadn't made sense in the
context of the conversation. This was during the early stages of
Eloise's obsession with Heddwen, and Meleri had been too fully
occupied trying to make sense of what was going on with the
Powells to pay much attention to it.

I said that at the beginning of my relationship with Eloise,
she seemed to be confusing Olivia and Heddwen. I was certain
I'd heard Eloise interchange Heddwen's and Olivia's names, but
now Eloise was adamant this wasn't the case.

'From what you're saying, I don't think this is multiple personalities,' Meleri said, 'because it's Heddwen and Olivia, not
Eloise and Olivia. Isn't it? She isn't changing into Olivia.' Meleri
looked over with alarm. '*Is* she? Wouldn't we have seen Eloise
"changing" into Olivia? Is that the word for it? "Changing"?
Wouldn't someone have caught her being Olivia before now?'

'That may have been what happened with the journal,' I said.
'For that moment, she *was* Olivia, and she couldn't help it. She
had to answer as Olivia.'

'Is multiple personalities even a thing?' Meleri asked. 'For real? I thought it had been written off as part of the 1990s, along with satanic cults and all that.'

This provoked a long tangential conversation about dissociative disorders. There was, indeed, a brief period when it had been a fashionable diagnosis, and it had always been a fertile area for sensationalized books and films. At the time this caused complicated issues for those who genuinely suffered from this disorder, in part because a kickback against the diagnosis soon followed, and professionals became reluctant to identify it as such, and in part because the real disorder was neither cool nor fun to live with.

There was a pause in our conversation.

One of the pub's claims to fame was that everything was freshly prepared, and this appeared to be code for 'we are truly very slow', because Meleri and I had been there almost an hour and nothing but our drinks had arrived at the table. Meleri excused herself to use the toilet.

I peered out the small window next to the table. The view across open moorland was made wobbly by the old glass. We were in the absolute middle of nowhere.

As I stared out the window, waiting for Meleri to return, my mind picked through the conversation. I felt a faint sense of betraying Eloise in telling Meleri about Olivia, in bringing up the prospect that Olivia was a genuine disorder. I *had* been here myself as a teenager. I had been through the longing for a world a little more magical, and possibly a little more controllable, than the one I had. I had been through the embarrassment of having to own up to an overactive imagination. I had been through the accusations of mental illness, of being 'weird' or 'not right in the head'. It was surprising at how unsettling such behaviour looked, now that I was on the other side of the table. It *was* weird. I didn't see any alternative to alerting Meleri and the others responsible for Eloise's welfare that something more serious might be going on, especially in light of the seriousness of her early abuse. But it still felt like a betrayal of trust.

When Meleri returned, I spoke of this with her. She, of course, felt my saying something was very much the right thing to do, and moved us on to a conversation about how Eloise could be further supported if it was confirmed she had a dissociative disorder. Treatment would be more or less what Eloise was already receiving: the group therapy programme at Cae Newydd, CBT, relaxation exercises and perhaps a referral for medication.

Meleri and I talked a little further about the situation, and then Meleri asked me about another child of hers I was working with, and we drifted off on a different train of conversation. Finally our food arrived.

Eloise was balancing the purple notebook on her knees. As I crossed the big room to the beanbag area, she smiled at me and waved, the first time I was given such a cheerful greeting since our rides to Pen-y-Garth.

'I did us tea, look?' she said, as I set my satchel down. There was a mug beside each beanbag.

'That's great. I really appreciate how you have everything ready for me when I come.'

'And I got this.' She held out the journal.

It took me a few moments to organize myself as I settled into the beanbag. I took out my own pen and notebook, and paused long enough to sip the tea. Eloise balanced the purple notebook precariously on one knee.

Reaching over for it, I opened the notebook and paged through to the current week.

Day One
Name the Event: Going to breakfast. Feeling: Angry. Because nobody had sympathy even though they should have. Response: I got cross. Is that what you planned or was it a reaction: Yes, because I'm not being treated nice. What was the outcome: I left them alone.

I looked over. 'Good for you! This is exactly what we've been trying to do. Let's look at what happened in a little more detail, so we can see how things fit together. This was last Wednesday, and you were feeling angry. Tell me a little more about what occurred to make you feel that way?'

'Oh, this isn't *me*,' Eloise said in a tone that implied I'd made a very basic mistake. 'Olivia filled in the journal this week. But I can tell you what happened. There, on Wednesday, she woke up feeling very poorly. She had a horrid cold, but she got up anyway. When she went in for breakfast, just as she was getting her porridge, she did this big sneeze. It wasn't her fault. It's never your fault if you sneeze when you have a cold. But everyone was, like, "Ewww! Get away from the food! Your boogers'll go all over my porridge!" That made her feel pissed off. I mean, she felt poorly anyway, and then everyone was rude to her.'

I paused.

Eloise paused too. She regarded me, her expression going from innocent engagement to wariness in a split second. 'You're going to say I shouldn't have done this, aren't you?' she said. Her voice sounded on the verge of tears.

'It sounds to me like you already know the answer to that. It isn't Olivia's journal, is it? It's yours.'

'I thought you said last time I could do it this way,' she replied in an offended tone. 'I thought that's what all that "I understand you" crap you said last week was about.'

I regarded her.

Eloise lowered her head and gave a small snuffle. Rubbing a hand over her nose, she lowered her head even further until it was almost against her chest.

'You're finding it very difficult to do this journal as yourself, aren't you?' I asked softly.

'I hate doing it as myself,' she replied.

'Why is that?'

'Because I hate myself. I hate thinking about myself. I hate being in my own mind.'

'It's more comfortable being Olivia?'

'I'm not *being* Olivia. I wish you'd stop saying that. I'm not some five-year-old, pretending. You said you had a person inside you, so I thought you knew better than to think that.'

'I apologize for stating it that way,' I said.

'It's more comfortable being *with* Olivia. I don't want to kill myself when I'm with Olivia. But I bloody well do all the rest of the time.'

'I'm sorry to hear you feel so unhappy.'

'Would you *stop* that? Would you quit saying you're sorry about everything I say?'

I closed my mouth.

'I *hate* myself!' Unexpectedly, she threw her head back and let out an anguished howl, then flung her hands up over her face. '*I hate myself!* Can't you understand that? I hate, hate, hate, hate, *hate* myself. I can't stand it! *I can't stand it!*' She tore at her skin.

Within seconds staff were there around us, taking hold of Eloise, restraining her. Two men and a woman. 'Calm down. Calm down. Calm down,' the woman was saying and this only made Eloise more distressed.

'Do you need something to help? Can you take a tablet?', one of the men said.

Eloise screamed incoherently.

The other man forcibly removed Eloise's hands from her face and pinned them to the side of her body. Together, they bundled her away.

I was caught completely off guard. Everything had happened so suddenly that I was left shocked, my heart racing in my throat.

Eloise was taken to the lockdown room to recover safely from her distressed feelings, but no one seemed to notice I was still there. I sat back down on the beanbag to gather my own thoughts, but when no one came over to me, I finally got up and went to the staff station to enquire about what was now best for me to do.

The woman behind the desk said that Eloise had been given diazepam and needed to stay in the safe room for half an hour to ensure she was fully calmed down.

'May I see her afterwards?' I asked.

'She'll be sleepy, I expect.'

I didn't mind that. It was more important to me not to leave on this note, so I asked if it was all right if I continued to wait over in the beanbag corner until Eloise was released.

'Suit yourself,' the woman said.

chapter twenty-two

Iain came out to me. 'It's time for Eloise's lunch,' he said. 'She doesn't feel like going to the dining room, so she'll have her lunch in the quiet suite. If you'd like to sit with her in there, you may.'

I followed him down a dim, narrow hallway to a small series of rooms. One was the lockdown room, with padded walls visible through the small glass window. Beside it were two smaller rooms, both painted pink. One had beanbag chairs and a rug. The other appeared to be a small kitchen with a sink, a single cupboard, a fridge and a table with two chairs. It was here that Eloise was sitting. A tray of food had been placed on the table in front of her. She looked surprised to see me.

'I didn't want to leave without saying goodbye. How are you feeling?' I asked, and pulled out the chair opposite her and sat down.

Eloise blew out a long breath. 'Tired.'

'I can imagine. Strong feelings are draining.'

She nodded.

A moment's silence passed and Eloise shoved the tray of food down the table.

'Aren't you hungry?' I asked.

She shook her head.

'A tuna sandwich with tomato. Perhaps if you ate just half, it would replenish your energy. It looks quite nice to me.'

'You can have it,' she said. Her tone was genuine.

'Thanks, but I think it's meant for you.'

'No, it's all right.'

I smiled. 'We'll just leave it there. Perhaps you'll feel like it soon.'

Then silence.

I hadn't been certain what I would do in going back to see her. Mostly I wanted to reassure her that her behaviour had not upset me, that while she had lost control, the world itself had remained stable, and I was still comfortable being with her. It was obvious she'd been drugged. There was an un-Eloise-like serenity about her.

I was wary of talking about the journal or Olivia, because I still wasn't completely clear what had set her off so abruptly, so I decided to try taking us in a different direction. I asked, 'What's been your most favourite thing that we've done together?'

Eloise considered a moment. I was expecting her usual shrug, but the medication seemed to have smoothed her responses, so she just sat, thinking for several moments.

'Going to Pen-y-Garth,' she said at last.

'I'm pleased to hear you enjoyed going there. What did you like best about it?'

'The drive, mostly. Because it was beautiful. And because you always talked to me properly then, and not like I'm a 'client'. That's when you first told me you had a person in your head like I did, and that felt good. I felt the best in the world, when you told me that.'

'I'm glad. I enjoyed that drive too,' I said.

She smiled self-consciously.

'What's been your least favourite thing?'

'Being here.'

'Yes, I can imagine. But I mean between us. Of the things we've done together.'

Eloise considered the question, then said, 'When you were upset with me at the eisteddfod. You didn't believe me when I told you I hadn't bitten Buddug. You believed Ffion and not me.'

'Should I have believed you?' I asked.

Eloise nodded. 'Yes, of course you should have, because I was telling the truth. I didn't bite Buddug. She bit herself. She was being super weird that day and did this little freak-out in the toilets and bit her own arm. I don't know why Ffion said it was me. But you believed her. You automatically assumed I was lying.'

This news surprised me. While the events had been confused in that way issues with kids can often be, I had had no reason to suspect Ffion would outright lie. Now the seeds of doubt were sown.

'I'm sorry if that's the case,' I said. 'I remember it a little differently, but if that is what truly happened, then I'm genuinely very sorry for not believing you.'

'It's okay. I got over it.'

'It's not okay. If you were innocent, I shouldn't have assumed.'

'No, it's okay.'

Silence again. Eloise looked around the small room and then reached over and snagged the plate with the tuna fish sandwich. She took half and began to eat it.

'I've an idea,' I said, and opened my satchel. Searching through, I pulled out the therapeutic game I'd been playing with my enrichment group the very first time Eloise had come to me. It consisted of little sticky labels with different emotions on them. To play the game, each person had an emotion label stuck to his or her forehead. The other players, who could see the label, acted out the emotion and the wearer tried to guess it. I lay the sheet down on the table.

Eloise's eyebrow quirked up. 'I don't think we can play that with just you and me.' Her tone was deadpan, which made it sound like she was being sarcastic, but I think the drugs were affecting her to the point that she was genuinely confused by my putting the game out.

'I want to play it a different way.' I reached in the satchel again and brought out a box of red and black draught pieces. I dumped them on the table.

The sheet had ten different emotional states listed, ranging from 'excited' and 'happy' to 'disgusted' and 'angry'. I dumped the draught pieces on the table and sorted them into piles of black and red. I pushed the red across the table to Eloise.

'Here's how we do it. We will ask each other questions about things we've experienced, and that person will answer by put-

238

ting pieces on all the emotions she felt during the event. The number of pieces we put on that emotion will indicate how strongly we felt it.

'Here's the story to show you how it works: We have a black cat that comes around our farm. He's a stray. He eats our cat's food and he chases her away from her favourite place to sit and sun herself. He tries to come in our house if we leave the back door ajar, and then he pees everywhere. We have enough cats, so I've tried to find him a good home because I don't want him at our house. Twice now I've taken him to live with someone else, and both times he has run away and come back to us. Then this morning, when I was coming to work, I saw that he had been hit and killed on the road.'

I turned the sheet with the list of emotions around so it was easy for Eloise to read. 'I'm going to use these draught pieces to show my feelings about this. I'm going to put four pieces on "sad", because I feel very sad that this cat was killed. I'm going to put one piece on "shocked", because I felt shock seeing him in the road. Because he's a stray, he's always walking along the road from farm to farm, and knows how to avoid cars, so I didn't expect him to be hit. And I'm going to put two on "confused", because he was a bother to me and I wanted to get rid of him, but not this way. I didn't want him to be killed. So now I wish he was still here, and that makes me confused.'

Eloise had listened intently to my tale.

'So, that's an example of what we're doing,' I said. 'So I'm going to ask the first question. How do you feel about doing the journal?'

239

Eloise leaned forward and stacked four draught pieces on 'confused' and nothing more.

'That's interesting. Why confused?'

'Because I don't know what to do.'

'You did a very good job with it this week,' I said. 'Or rather, Olivia did. But you clearly understood it.'

'Olivia understood it.'

'Okay,' I replied, not wanting to invalidate her feelings and not wanting to invite Olivia back into the conversation quite yet. 'Many times we have more than one feeling about a situation. Like I did with the cat. I felt sad and shocked and confused all at the same time. You feel confused about the journal. Do you have any other feelings?'

She studied the sheet carefully for several moments. At last she reached for the draught pieces and stacked four on 'angry'.

'Okay, good. Thank you. Can you tell me what makes you feel angry about it?'

'That I don't understand it.'

'I think we may need another emotion on this list,' I said, 'because I'm hearing another feeling coming out of your confusion and anger.' I tore a strip of paper off my notebook and wrote 'frustration' on it and put it alongside the others. 'What you're feeling is frustration, isn't it? Frustration is that annoyed feeling we get when we can't accomplish something we want to.'

Eloise nodded. Then she looked over at me. 'My turn to ask a question now. What do *you* feel about the journal?'

I grinned and scooped up my draught pieces. Leaning forward, I considered the list. 'About six pieces on "frustrated". But

I think we need yet another emotion that isn't there: "interested".' I wrote it down and set the slip of paper beside the others. 'Because while I'm feeling frustrated that we're not making very good progress with the journal, I also feel interested to see what happens with it each week. I like doing it with you.'

Eloise smiled.

'Next question,' I said. 'What do you feel about letting Olivia do the journal instead of doing it yourself?'

'We're missing another word,' Eloise replied. '"Like".'

'I'm not sure "like" is an emotion,' I said. 'Perhaps "happy"?'

'Of course "like" is an emotion,' Eloise countered. 'I like something. It doesn't mean I'm happy.'

'Emotions are feelings. You can say, "'I attempted to control my emotions." "I attempted to control my frustration." "I attempted to control my anger." "I attempted to control my excitement." But you wouldn't say, "I attempted to control my like,"' I replied.

'What a silly way to make a definition!' she said, and laughed. 'And I'm sure I can control my like. So give me some paper so I can add it.'

I was pleased at this reaction. Not only did it tell me that Eloise understood the point of what we were doing, but she seemed to have overridden her usual resistance to participation. Her delight in taking me on was obvious.

Putting the bit of paper with 'like' written on it beside the others, Eloise put five draught pieces on the word.

'So you really like Olivia filling out the journal for you?'

She nodded. 'It isn't boring then. We ought to have "boring" on that list. Let me make a piece of paper with that on.'

'You do understand that the point of the journal is to become aware of what's happening in your thoughts. *Your* thoughts,' I said, as she wrote out another slip with 'boring' on it.

'Well, Olivia is part of my thoughts, isn't she?' Eloise replied. 'Isn't that what you said?'

No way to argue that.

She looked up at me. 'It's boring in my own head. If the question you asked was: how does it feel to be in Eloise's head, I would put, like, ten pieces on "boring" and two on "sad" and . . . maybe six on "frustrated". And then I'd need some more pieces. Your pieces, maybe, so I could put, like, five on "angry" and . . . and . . . we're missing some more words here, but I can't think what they are.'

'You've got quite a lot of emotion going on inside your head, don't you?' I said quietly.

'Yep,' she replied curtly.

A pause.

Eloise sat back and looked at the sheet of sticky-backed emotions and the several scraps of paper beside them that held the emotions we'd added. 'This would look nicer if we redid it,' she said. 'I wish we had some of that coloured paper like we used at Pen-y-Garth. And a measuring stick. If we had that, I could make this into a proper game.'

'That's a good idea,' I said.

'You know, this *could* be a proper game. Maybe we could create it and sell it and make, like, lots of money!'

I grinned at her unexpectedly entrepreneurial spirit.

Eloise leaned forward again. 'Anyway, it's my turn to ask you a question. How would you feel if I told you something really bad?'

'That's a bit too general for me to answer,' I replied. 'What did you have in mind?'

'Well, like, if I told you I killed someone, how would you feel?'

'*Have* you killed someone?' I asked.

'Well, if I had, how would you put your draught pieces down?' she asked.

'I think I would need to know more first. For example, if you killed someone because they were trying to kill you first, I would feel differently than I would if I found out you'd killed someone because you thought it would be good fun to kill someone. And I'd feel differently still if you'd killed someone accidentally. There are too many variables to give one answer.'

'What if, say, like, someone killed a child? Like, maybe it wasn't on purpose, but maybe it was? How would you feel?'

I regarded her. She met my eyes in a steady gaze.

Pulling over my draught pieces, I stacked them up. 'Sad. About six pieces on "sad". And "angry". The other six pieces there. And I think we're missing another word. "Horrified". And "shocked". I'd have to borrow some of yours so that I could put pieces on those too.' I looked up. 'How would you put your pieces down?'

Eloise pushed aside my draught pieces. Picking up one of

hers, she let it hover over several different emotions before finally dropping it on 'sad', but even then she didn't let go of it. 'You know, the truth is, I'd feel all these emotions. All of them put together. All the bad ones.'

'What child do you have in mind?' I asked.

'My brother.'

'You feel he was killed?'

'Mrs Thomas always tells me I don't remember. She says I was too little and that it has to be a dream or something that's got confused with my memories, but she isn't right. I remember my brother very clearly. He had brown curly hair. His name was Jacob. It was Christmastime. There was a big Christmas tree in the sitting room and he was looking at the baubles and our mum got cross, because he kept touching them. She said he'd break them. He had his hands around this blue bauble. I can remember that, how he grabbed it because it was like a little ball, and my mum – I think it was my mum and not Paul – that was her boyfriend then, but I think it was her – threw this hair brush at my brother. Threw it at him to get him to let go of the bauble, but it hit him on the head and he fell backwards. He still had the bauble in his hands. He didn't let go of it when it fell, so the whole tree came over with him. It hit me. I remember that, because this swoosh of branches came down over my head and it hurt. And Jacob hit his head on the edge of the coal hod. And he was dead.'

'Wow,' I said. 'What an awful thing to happen.'

'I have nightmares about it. There's always Christmas baubles in it. Sometimes they're falling. Sometimes they're chasing me. Even now, I wake up screaming.'

She pulled the sheet with the emotion stickers on it closer and examined it. 'Probably if I had to do this, I'd put, like, the entire stack of draught pieces on "scared". I'd put all mine on there because it was the scariest thing that ever happened to me. Mrs Thomas says it's a false memory, and that my brother didn't die then. She said he didn't die until I was almost five, but I don't believe her, because I can see it so clearly. I can see him lying there, that blue bauble still in his hands, and his head was cracked open and the hod was all bloody. So then I'd take your draught pieces and put two of them on "disgusted" because that was a disgusting scene. And then I'm going to use your "horrified" and put three pieces on that. And then "surprised", I'll put three on "surprised", because that's how I felt. And then "confused". I'll put all the rest on "confused".'

Her body bent forward, her head down as if she were reading a complex text, Eloise studied the sheet of paper with the emotion stickers. Silence fell around us.

'Yes,' she said in a thoughtful tone. 'I think that's good.' She looked over at me. 'That's how I would do it.'

chapter twenty-three

Arranging to meet Meleri later that afternoon, I told her about my time with Eloise, about her sudden anger, her spell in lock-down and our impromptu game with the draught pieces.

As a charity volunteer, I did not have clearance to read the Social Services files of the children I worked with in the normal course of things, so I'd not seen them for myself. Up to that point, I worked from summaries provided by Meleri and Sue-Pugh. Now, however, it was time to have accurate details. In particular, I wanted to find out precisely what had happened with her brother.

Meleri had Eloise's file on her desk, or rather, files, because it no longer fitted in one. The stack was literally six inches thick. As a writer, used to estimating number of words and number of pages, I reckoned Eloise had had the equivalent of two books written about her.

'I know what you heard,' Meleri said. 'She gave you that story about the Christmas bauble, didn't she? I don't know how she's come to have that in her head, but it isn't true.'

There was a marker put inside one of the files to indicate

where the account of Eloise's brother had been recorded in her file and Meleri handed it over to me. Laying it down on the desk, I opened it.

His name *was* Jacob. That much was accurate. He had been abused, but the records indicated it was as a baby, when he'd been shaken so severely that he suffered permanent brain damage. As a consequence he was unable to walk or talk, and was confined to a wheelchair.

'So, see?' Meleri said, 'that can't be an actual memory. I know it seems very real to Eloise, but then so does Olivia.'

'Who else could it be?' I asked. 'Her sister? Could this have happened to her sister? She was abused as well, wasn't she? Isn't that why she eventually ended up for adoption?'

'I don't think so. There's no record of anything. She went out of the system at five. An English couple adopted her and she seemed to settle well with them. They moved back to the Home Counties not long after, so we no longer have contact.'

'Why on earth was Eloise left behind?'

'All the kids had different fathers. We could terminate the rights in Evie's case, but Eloise's dad kept wanting another chance. His convictions have been endless, but they were never very serious. Once she was in her new relationship, Mum thought she could cope with Eloise.'

'Was that Darren?'

Meleri nodded.

'We all know how well that worked out.'

*

My next port of call was with Sue-Pugh, because I wanted to check back through our notes on the investigation into Eloise's behaviour at Pen-y-Garth. Eloise had maintained her innocence all the way through. I would have expected her to deny culpability when first confronted, because she didn't like admitting to being wrong even in insignificant situations, but it seemed odd to me that she was still so adamant. At the time, I felt certain that she had been guilty because I'd seen her short temper with Buddug on other occasions, but also because I had no reason to think Ffion would have lied about something like this. Ffion wasn't a perfect child by any means, but she was your ordinary, happy-go-lucky six-year-old, and I had never seen any inclination towards vindictiveness. Now, however, seeds of doubt had been sown.

Sue-Pugh was touchingly pleased to see me. She made us tea and took down her biscuit box. Sitting me down at the small table in her office, she wanted an update on all the news. When I asked her about the Pen-y-Garth investigation, she was surprised.

'Of course Eloise is going to maintain her innocence,' Sue-Pugh said with an emphatic swoop of tone. 'She wants to look good in your eyes. Of course she'd never admit to having done it.'

I explained that I did rather think by this point Eloise would admit to it, if it were true, as it was well after the fact. I found Eloise capable of considerable honesty when she wasn't feeling threatened. Were we *sure* she was guilty?

'Of course we are!'

Oddly, Sue-Pugh being so sure made me feel more doubtful,

not less. I asked if she would mind if I went through the notes again, just for my own satisfaction.

Sue-Pugh rifled through her file cabinet until she found the appropriate papers.

I read through what we had recorded: Ffion had told me what had happened while the school eisteddfod was still in progress. I had looked at the bite mark on Buddug's arm, which was quite indistinct. It was clearly an injury but not entirely apparent it was a bite mark. I had confronted Eloise. Eloise had denied it. Ffion told me that Eloise had also pinched Buddug and other children, including her. During the follow-up investigation, Bethan said that Eloise had flicked Ffion with her finger.

I sat back. According to Ffion Eloise had bitten Buddug and pinched her. According to Bethan, Buddug had had a tantrum, and Eloise had flicked her finger against Ffion's head. Bethan hadn't seen who did the biting.

Could Eloise be innocent? I was horrified that so many of us had assumed Ffion's version of the story was true. Shock had been my initial reaction when Buddug had turned up with the bite mark. It never crossed my mind at the time to question if Ffion was telling the truth or not, and this, of course, may have influenced the other adults' point of view.

So who did bite whom? Who pinched? Who flicked? Was it as Ffion had said? Or had Ffion not seen what happened and it somehow looked to her as if Eloise had done it? Or was she piqued because she'd been flicked and wanted to blame Eloise? Why had she said 'pinched' and not 'flicked'? Was this an English/Welsh confusion? Or a misunderstanding about what

had happened? Was Ffion embroidering the incident or report-
ing it?

The whole matter bothered me deeply, but I wasn't sure
what to do about it. As far as Sue-Pugh was concerned the
investigation wasn't worth reopening at this stage, so there
wasn't going to be a definitive answer.

The only person I could think to talk it over with was Lynn,
my charity supervisor. I think part of my desire to talk to Lynn
was born from the need to apologize to her, or perhaps 'apologize' was the wrong word. To acknowledge her wisdom. The
stand-out moment in my relationship with Lynn had been that
time she'd pulled me up for assuming I knew her children went
to the local school. At the time I'd felt humiliated by her rebuke.
Now, suddenly, all I could think was: *Lynn was right to correct
me*. Assumption is dangerous. I felt the need to tell her I had
finally learned.

As is always the case with wise teachers, Lynn listened with
kindness and sympathy as I unravelled this tortuous tale, and
there was no intimation that I should have known better. Did
she think Eloise was innocent? No way to say, she replied. What
did she think I should do? There was a long pause. Then Lynn
said she agreed with Sue-Pugh, that it would probably be
unhelpful at this time to go further with it. It was water under
the bridge as far as the children at Pen-y-Garth were concerned.
She suggested I talk it over further with Eloise, show my support, acknowledge I didn't have all the facts and, if Eloise felt
heard, leave it there.

*

When I came out to see Eloise on Thursday, she was waiting on the beanbag chairs. As I came over to sit down, she said, 'I asked Iain if we could use the table in the quiet suite again, and he said we could as long as no one was in lockdown. Do you want to?'

Surprised at this initiative on Eloise's part, I nodded. 'All right.'

'I like it better back here,' she said, as we entered the small room with the table. She lay the journal down and pulled a chair out. 'It's calmer. Sitting at the table makes it easier for me to think.'

I sat down in the chair opposite. 'So, who's written the journal this week? You or Olivia?'

'Remember that game we played last week? I thought about other words that should go in it, and I've written them down.' She opened the journal to the back page. 'Here are some of them. "Guilty". That's a feeling, hey? And "shame". And "sorry". Do you think "sorry" is different from "guilty"? I've been thinking about that, and I can't decide, but I think it is.'

I nodded. 'Yes, I agree. It's different.'

'They're really close, those feelings. "Guilty" and "ashamed". We have a group counselling session on Saturday afternoons, and Michael, who's the counsellor, was talking about feeling guilty and feeling ashamed, so that's when I decided we should put them in our game.'

Pleased that she was making these connections, I agreed with her.

'And what's the name of the feeling you get when something ends?'

'Loss?' I said.

Eloise considered this. 'Hmmm. That's a feeling too, but it's not the one I'm thinking of. What I'm thinking of is the feeling you get when you miss something. It's ended and you miss it. Loss is, like, well, *loss*. Losing something. I'm meaning when it's already gone and you miss it.'

'Can you give me an example?' I asked.

'When we went to Pen-y-Garth, you would drive up over that one big hill outside Llanfair and we'd see the mountains. I miss that. When I think about it I get a missing kind of feeling about us going to Pen-y-Garth and I feel sad. What's that called?'

'"Nostalgia", maybe?'

'"Nostalgia",' Eloise repeated carefully, as if she were tasting the word. '"Nostalgia". We need to put that word on our list too.'

'May I see your journal?' I held my hand out.

She slid it out of my reach. 'I didn't do it.'

'Did Olivia do it?'

'No. Because let's play our game instead. I liked that. I like it, because I get to ask you questions as well. I'm fed up with doing the journal.' Her face brightened. '"Fed up". That's another feeling to add to our list!'

I was realizing I'd created something of a monster with this game.

'I tried to get some paper to make our game up nicely, so we'd have it for real,' Eloise said. 'I wanted to surprise you with it. But they wouldn't let me. There's not much you can do in here unless they tell you to do it.'

I opened my satchel to take out the draught pieces and the paper list from the previous visit. Eloise added her new words to the list in careful script.

'I get to ask first,' she said, 'because I'm the one who said to play the game.'

Stacking my draught pieces up, I nodded. 'All right.'

'How do you feel if people make you do stuff that you don't want to do?' she asked.

I put two draught pieces on 'angry'. '"Angry" is not quite the right word,' I said. '"Cross" would be closer, because it doesn't imply that you are seriously upset. I think we all feel a bit cross when someone makes us do stuff we don't want to do. But . . .'

'But what?'

'I'd want to know why the person wanted me to do whatever it was I didn't want to do. Maybe they were trying to boss me. That's what it always feels like at first when someone tells you to do something, doesn't it? So it's natural to feel cross. But maybe, in fact, they were trying to help me. Maybe they wanted me to learn something that would make my life easier.'

'You're going teacher on me,' Eloise said, a faint exasperation in her tone.

'Maybe that's because I am a teacher,' I replied with a smile. 'So I'm always going to be thinking about learning things.'

'Yeah, it's how you get boring too. I didn't mean like how a teacher tells you stuff you don't want to do. I mean, what if your whole life is about other people making you do stuff you don't want to do?'

'Is that how it feels to you?' I asked.

'Yes.' She put a stack of draught pieces on 'anger'. Then she reached for the pen and paper. 'There. There's "fed up", because we definitely need that.' She slid the draught pieces down from 'anger'. 'I'm fed up with my life.'

I put a couple of my draught pieces on 'sad'. 'We're missing another word,' I said. ' "Helpless".'

'Yes. "*Helpless*". That's good,' said Eloise, as if I were the student and she were the teacher. She added that to the list.

I put the rest of my draught pieces there. 'Is that how it feels? Do we have it right?'

Eloise surveyed the paper and the pieces.

A moment's silence. Just a pause, the sort that comes naturally in the middle of active interaction when one stops to assess a situation, but then it grew. Eloise was poised over the paper with all its feelings, her muscles tense, her expression frozen, anticipation of further movement hanging, suspended in the air. Then slowly, as the silence drew out, her posture relaxed. She tipped her head and continued to regard our shabby little game.

'Know why I like this?' she murmured at the paper. 'Because I don't know how else to say what I feel. Except to move these little marker things around on the paper. I don't know how else to say it.'

I looked at her.

'This is like one of those . . . disabled boards, you know? Like Stephen Hawking had, where he pointed at letters and it made speech for him. I don't know how I feel unless I put a marker thing on it. That's how I feel.'

She let out a long breath. 'Nobody here wanted to know about this game when I tried to tell them. Micha, this girl whose room is near mine, she thought I was talking about doing a Ouija board. She thought you and me were doing Ouija, and she said to me how creepy that was. She told me I shouldn't work with you any more.'

I laughed. 'This isn't a Ouija board, is it? It's just a list of feelings, and seeing them written down helps clarify what they are. That's a good thing, and I'm glad it helps you express what's going on inside. It's all right to need them written down. I think a lot of people are that way. I'm sorry Micha and the others weren't interested.'

Eloise smoothed the board out between us. She slid more draught pieces onto 'helpless' until there was a stack of six or seven. The rest she moved to 'angry', and then she began to shift the pieces around, some on this emotion, some on that. We were no longer distinguishing between her colour and mine, because twelve draught pieces didn't seem sufficient to express the complex feelings Eloise was experiencing. It looked less like a Ouija board and more like some strange kind of poker game, as Eloise kept rearranging the pieces, moving them from emotion to emotion, adding pieces to some stacks, removing from other stacks. Sad, scared, helpless, hurt, angry, fed up, frustrated, all took their turns.

Eloise did not speak as she moved the pieces around. The activity had so absorbed her that it seemed almost as if she were completing a complex puzzle. As she continued, I noticed her muscles slowly relax. The tight posture at the beginning loosened. At last she stopped. One draught piece was on 'trapped', one was on 'lost', a few were sitting at the side of the paper, all the rest were on 'sad'.

She looked up at me and smiled. 'I love you.'

chapter twenty-four

The next Thursday, Eloise was back on the beanbags, waiting for me. She had the journal balanced on her knee.

'I went to Youth Court on Monday,' she announced, as I sat down. 'I've put it in the journal. I've said how it made me feel. *Awful*. I hated it. There was this lady magistrate. She had this minging hairstyle. Honestly, it made her look like an SS officer. All she needed was a little spike sticking out of her skull. I've wrote it all down, so that you can't accuse me of not doing my journal.'

Although I'd known the court date was coming up, I hadn't been informed of when it was exactly and felt a little disappointed that Meleri had not thought to tell me. I now realized this went some way in explaining Eloise's difficult behaviour in our previous few meetings.

'What came of the hearing?' I asked.

'I have to stay here for two months more. Then maybe I can go back to a foster home.' Eloise was speaking breezily, as if this were no big deal.

'Did you come away from the hearing clear about every-thing?' I asked.

'You think I'm stupid, don't you?' she said, annoyed.

'No. I simply want to know if everything was clear. I'm here to help and it isn't easy to do that without knowing what you know. Or for that matter, what's going on. Mrs Thomas didn't tell me it was this week.'

'Well, I just told you. I don't know what there's not to get about it. I was in court because I broke into the Powells' house and caused damage.'

'What were your feelings around breaking into the Powells' house?'

'They didn't ask me that.'

'No, I'm asking.'

She shrugged. 'Felt like it. I don't know. It was ages ago now.'

I rummaged in my satchel and pulled out the sheet of feel-ings and the draught pieces. I lay them on the floor beside the beanbag.

'I don't want to do that,' Eloise said. 'That really is a stupid game, if you think about it. It's *juvenile*.'

'It was helpful last week.'

'Yeah, well, this isn't last week, is it?'

'Let's just see if we can use it,' I said, and picked up a draught piece. 'You said you broke into the Powells' house because you felt like it. What feelings were going on that made that seem like a good idea?'

'This isn't how my session with you is supposed to go, you know,' Eloise said. 'You are here to do the journal with me. I do the group therapy with Michael to talk about feelings. That's what we do there. We sit around and Michael makes us talk about our feelings. The magistrate said that's good enough and if I'm here another two months, then I can go to a foster home. I don't need to do reparations. She said it's too long past to do reparations.'

'This isn't about reparations, Eloise. I'm asking you what your feelings were when you broke into the Powells' house,' I replied. I put a handful of draught pieces in her lap.

'I *don't* have to do this. You're just here as a befriender. You really can't make me do anything.'

'That's true. But I want you to do it anyway. Just to help me understand.'

Eloise drew in a long, noisy breath. 'Well, I'm not going to.'

I settled back in the beanbag and didn't say anything. Eloise didn't speak again either and the minutes began to draw out between us. I passed the time consciously relaxing my muscles one by one, because I found them unexpectedly tense.

When nothing more was forthcoming, I finally said, 'I remember way, way, way back in the beginning when you first came to me. You told me how nice Heddwen was to you when you first went to the Powells'.'

'Yes, what of it?' I could still hear annoyance in Eloise's voice that I assumed came from being forced to have a conversation she didn't want.

'What was the nicest thing about Heddwen?'

'I don't know.'

I didn't respond.

'I said I don't know.'

I continued my silence.

'I *don't* know.'

'Can you remember the day you arrived?'

'No,' Eloise said.

Realizing I wasn't going to get anywhere with this, I reached out my hand for the journal. 'So let's have a go with this. Who's done it this time? You or Olivia?'

'You make me feel about six years old when you say "You or Olivia". It's, like, in this patronizing tone of voice that makes it sound like I still play make-believe. I hate it when you do that. It makes me not want to fill in your stupid journal at all.'

'I'm sorry,' I said in as quiet a tone as I could muster, 'because I don't mean it like that at all. It was just a question.'

I flipped open the journal.

One: Event that happened. Had to go to Youth Court.

Two: Name the Feeling. Hate. Hate. Hate. Hate. Like I want to murder someone.

Three: What did you do? Did what they told me. Like I didn't murder anyone, which I felt like doing, but didn't.

Four: Is that what you intended to do? I didn't have any choice.

Five: What happened next? I came back to Shithole.

Eloise was watching me closely as I read. 'See?' she said with relish. 'I filled it out just as you said.'

'Well, yes. You filled it out . . .'

With no warning whatsoever, Eloise exploded. I hadn't been looking at her, as I had my head down to read the journal. I was trying to think what to say next in order to draw together what she had written, and was just taking a pause, so she caught me entirely off guard.

'*I hate this!*' She suddenly screamed. 'I hate this! I hate this stupid journal!' And abruptly she snatched the journal from my lap and pitched it across the room. 'I hate this fucking place! I hate you! I hate *everything*. Hate! Hate! *Hate!*' As she spoke her arms went around herself in a frenzied grasp, and I could see her fingers beginning to scrabble at her skin.

Once again, staff quickly appeared on the scene, surrounding Eloise. Within moments she was gone.

Feeling momentarily overwhelmed, I sank back down onto the beanbag. No doubt Eloise was on edge from the court appearance, but it was dispiriting to see her become so unexpectedly agitated. There were no lockdown rooms in the healthy outer world that I so longed for her to rejoin.

As with the previous occasion, I waited until Iain came to tell me Eloise was out of the lockdown, and once again we found ourselves at the small table, a sad-looking ham sandwich between us.

'Do you suppose we could have a cup of tea?' I asked Iain.

He nodded.

Eloise accepted the tea without comment. She was quiet by

this point, an after-storm exhaustion and probably Valium weighing down her limbs. I stirred my tea and sipped it. Several minutes passed with us doing nothing more.

'It's been a rough few days, hasn't it?' I said.

Eloise nodded.

'It must have been hard, going over all that again.'

Another nod.

Silence. Eloise kept her head down.

'I didn't mean to do it,' she said at last. I didn't know what she was referring to, whether it was her explosion in the day room, or what had happened at the Powells' or something else.

'I'm sorry I shouted at you,' she said.

'That's all right.'

'It was because I want to talk to you about Olivia . . . but I don't want to talk to you about Olivia. I don't want you to think I'm mental. And I don't want them to know.' She nodded her head back towards the staff station. 'They *would* think I was mental, if they found out about Olivia. I'd be in here forever. Because they wouldn't understand.'

'I can understand,' I said softly.

'I want to tell you something,' Eloise murmured.

'Okay.'

'Looking at Heddwen Powell is like looking at Olivia.'

'I see.'

'Heddwen has the same sort of mouth. It's a big mouth, a mouth that smiles with teeth, like this.' Eloise drew back her lips without looking at me. 'And the way Heddwen's face is, when she turns it. It's Olivia's face.'

'I can see why that must have made Heddwen feel very special to you,' I said.

'Yes. Do you think it makes me sound nuts?'

'No, but it does help me understand where your feeling were coming from.'

Eloise fell silent, her head down.

The silence lasted so long that I began considering directions I could take that might further the conversation, but I couldn't find a good way to segue into other topics, so we just sat, studying our empty mugs.

'This one night . . .' she started, '. . . it was about . . . well, like, a month after I came. I had a nightmare. I can still remember it. I can remember exactly what I dreamt, because it was so awful. I was with my mum and we were in a shopping street somewhere. It was, like, a busy street, the kind you get at the seaside with lots of stuff hanging off the shopfronts. Suddenly at the corner behind us I saw this black-and-white monster. Mum had hold of my hand, and we started running to get away. She was dragging me down the street because, in the dream, I was little and I couldn't run fast enough. Then suddenly there was this cliff, and down below we could see the beach and the sea. Mum said we had to get down there to be safe. It was so steep, but she said we had to climb down, and she helped me over the edge. She was holding on to me by my hand, but I was too scared to move because it was so steep. Mum kept shouting to hurry up because the monster was almost there. Then suddenly the ground gave way under my feet. It just crumbled and Mum was screaming at me for being so stupid to slip, but it was scared screaming, the kind you do when you get angry because you're so frightened. And that was because she knew she couldn't hang on to me. She knew she'd lost me. I slipped out of her hand and started falling and falling, and I knew I was going to die.'

Eloise paused. 'Heddwen woke me up. Then, when she got me awake, she put her arms around me and cuddled me. I couldn't stop shaking. She said I could get in bed with her then, if I wanted. I got in and she wrapped her arms around me and we laid there cuddling.'

'How did that make you feel?' I asked.

'It was wonderful,' Eloise said.

'You just cuddled? Heddwen put her arms around you and held you? Did she do anything else?'

'She just held me. I felt so happy. I don't remember my mum ever cuddling me. She always got cross with me if I woke up at night. But I don't think I would have liked it if my mum had tried. She wasn't really like a mother, if I'm honest. It was more like I was her mother. If anything needed to be done, I did it, unless she had a man and then he did it. She never really took care of herself and she certainly didn't take care of me.'

'That must have been hard on you,' I said, 'because you were a little child then. Children need to be cared for.'

Eloise nodded. 'I took care of Evie.'

'You were just little. Too little for that responsibility. You needed someone to take care of you.'

Eloise shrugged.

'I expect that's why it felt so good when Heddwen responded

that way. You needed someone to take care of you because you were scared.'

Eloise sucked her lower lip in under her teeth and was thoughtful a long moment, and then she said, 'No. It was because it was as if Olivia had her arms around me. I was feeling her flesh, but it was like Olivia was suddenly real. Olivia holding me. It was like my best dream came true.'

'I can imagine that would be a powerful feeling,' I said.

'I wanted it to be that way forever,' she said softly. 'It was like you were telling me about, when you wanted to go into the world where your person was. Suddenly it was real and that was the best feeling I ever had, and I wanted it to last forever.'

'Did you tell Heddwen any of this?'

'No, of course not,' Eloise said. 'I didn't want her to think I was mental. I wouldn't be telling you, except that you said you understood this.'

'Yes. I can appreciate how special that must have felt to have Heddwen be so like Olivia, to have it feel as if Olivia had come to life.'

Eloise nodded.

A small silence drifted in around us.

'Do you think I *am* mental?' she asked softly.

'No,' I said.

'Other people do. Mrs Thomas and Sue-Pugh, both of them. And the magistrates at Youth Court. Basically, everyone except you.'

'I don't think you're mental, because I believe you are aware enough of the fact that Heddwen isn't Olivia that you are able to decide not to go to the Powells'.'

'Then how come I do keep doing it?' she asked.

'I don't know. Why do you think?' I asked.

'I don't know.'

There was a long pause. Eloise picked at her lip, pulling it out.

'I kept doing it because . . . I wanted Heddwen to put her arms around me again. I wanted her to keep touching me like that.'

'I see.'

'Do you think I'm gay?'

'Did you want her to touch you sexually?'

Again the thoughtful pause. 'No. I just wanted to be cuddled. I wanted to be touched like that, like someone cared how I felt.' She sighed heavily. 'So I tried to make it happen again. That's what got me in trouble. I pretended to have nightmares, but Heddwen never did that again. It was always Mum Powell who came. She would sit with me and talk to me, but that made me feel cross. I wanted Olivia . . .'

Eloise drained her tea, tipping it right back to get the last drops. 'Sometimes I pretended to hurt myself, because I thought maybe Heddwen would take care of me then. I did hurt myself this one time. It was just me and her at home, and I kept going out in the garden and stepping on the rake until finally it went in my foot.'

'You set up a lot of situations, didn't you?' I said.

'I thought it would get her to put her arms around me again.

But she didn't. Most of the time, she treated me like I was invisible.'

'I expect your actions may have frightened Heddwen a little, because she didn't know what the story was behind them. I'm sorry you needed something so much and it didn't happen,' I said.

Eloise nodded. 'I'm sorry too.'

chapter twenty-five

Back to Meleri.

The day was overcast, one of those gloomy, wet, late autumn afternoons where night starts filling up the crevices before the work day is over. Sitting in the wan fluorescence of Meleri's office, I nursed an insipid mug of instant coffee, a lukewarm, grey-brown liquid that tasted of almost nothing but was nonetheless welcoming simply because it was warm.

The conversation Eloise and I had had was so densely packed with information that I sought Meleri out, not only for her advice but also just to be able to think aloud.

Here at last was the connection between Heddwen and the imaginary Olivia. Having no consistent, predictable people in her chaotic young life, Eloise had created her own source of comfort, embodied in the fantasy figure of Olivia. Then, unexpectedly, there was Olivia in real life, responding in a kind, comforting way to Eloise's distress. Knowing this made sense of Eloise's stalking behaviour. Indeed, I found myself empathizing with the needy desperation that must have fuelled it. No, it was not at all appropriate, but I could imagine the joy she'd have experienced of having such deep needs met, and the longing she must have felt to repeat it.

Meleri heard different things in the story. 'What strikes me first,' she said, 'is the possibility of sexual abuse on the part of Heddwen. This sixteen-year-old girl, as she was then, took a thirteen-year-old into bed with her? To cuddle?

'The second thing are the sexual overtones in reverse. Eloise was trying to get this cuddling to happen again and, as we know, she has been incredibly persistent. There's a strong positive association between sexual abuse in childhood and same-sex sexuality in adulthood. How much of this "need to be cuddled" is the trauma of her childhood resurfacing, and how much is Eloise's own sexuality awakening? Up until now, Eloise has been quite asexual for her age. I've been noticing this for a while. With her, there's never talk about who she fancies at school or pictures of boy bands or TV stars on her bedroom wall. But I get a vibe off these conversations about Heddwen that is almost romantic . . . do you get that? In the back of my mind is the thought that this may be how she is channelling her sexual feelings.'

I told Meleri that Eloise had asked me outright whether I thought she was gay. I had demurred at the time, because I did not think it was appropriate that I make that judgement, but I too had sensed an aura of sexuality in what she was telling me. As far as Heddwen was concerned, I didn't know. It was possible that taking Eloise into her bed had been innocent and that there was no sexual contact. It was also possible that sexual overtones were coming from Eloise rather than Heddwen, so I didn't want to speculate at this stage. I also didn't want to lose the focus on Eloise. The issue wasn't only that Heddwen might be a sexual predator but also that Eloise was a vulnerable girl in early adolescence for whom even innocent affection would make a powerful impact. The physical comfort did not fill her up so much as make her aware of how empty she was. The overlay of an imaginary superhero added a complexity to the relationship between Heddwen and Eloise that couldn't be sustained.

Our conversation drifted into treatment and resolution. There would need to be a semi-formal investigation of Heddwen. Not formal at this point, as no allegations had been made, but Meleri wanted to talk both with Mr and Mrs Powell and with Heddwen to get a better sense of what was going on, and there would be a review of the other children who had been placed in the home.

I felt a twinge of sadness listening to Meleri lay out plans, because these were the times we were in as a society, always suspicious of the worst, never trusting innocence. This may well have been a case of two girls in bed together, one comforting the other after a nightmare, and nothing more, yet we had to jump through all the abuse investigation hoops, which were mildly traumatizing in themselves. I was sad this was so. I was sadder yet that there were so many good reasons why we had to do it.

Dealing with this side of things was straightforward. What we should now do with Eloise, not so much.

'How far do you think she's come?' Meleri asked, referring to Eloise's mental health. 'Do you think she's beginning to have insight into why she was stalking Heddwen? In a substantial way?'

I shook my head. 'I don't know. I do know she needs therapy. Proper talking therapy.'

'Yes. Her and about 50 million other kids in my care,' Meleri said. 'Unfortunately, for the time being, the best she'll get is the group therapy at Cae Newydd. That said, he's a good egg, the bloke who runs it. And he knows his stuff.'

I nodded.

'But do you think she's got insight?' Meleri asked again.

'Do you mean, does she understand that she needs to stop it?' I asked. 'Yes.'

'Do you think we'll be able to trust her on release?' Meleri asked.

'I hope so.'

A pause.

Meleri got up and took her mug to the small table at the back of the room where the electric kettle was. She looked over at me and held her mug up, a silent gesture asking if I wanted another drink. I shook my head.

When she returned to her seat, she said, 'I'm asking, because we've had something else come up.' She looked over at me. 'Eloise's dad is petitioning to take her.'

Surprised, I straightened up my chair. 'I thought he was in prison.'

'He was, but he's out again. He's been out a while, and he claims he's turned his life completely around. He's in a job. He's got a new wife and a small child. Now he wants to give Eloise a home.'

'Wow, that was fast. How . . .' I was genuinely shocked by this revelation, not only of the speed at which Eloise's father seemed to have accomplished it all, but also by the fact that Meleri was clearly taking this petition seriously.

'I know,' she said to my unasked question. 'It didn't work out last time, but that was quite a dodgy set-up. He was living with his mum. He wasn't in work. This time he's completed rehab properly, and he feels it's going to stick. He credits his success to this new woman. He says she's helped him commit to staying clean. He wants to be a good influence for his little boy.'

'Wow,' I said again, because this did astonish me. I shook my head. 'While that all sounds nice in theory, it sounds wrong to me in practice. Eloise hated being with her grandmother. She found the whole situation upsetting, if not downright trau-matic. I can't imagine she'd want to get into it again.'

'Yes, I know,' Meleri said. 'And this is still early days, so maybe it will come to nothing. But at the same time, we need to be realistic. Eloise is fifteen. She has her review meeting next sum-mer to discuss her future, and we want to try and keep her in education, if we can, but she's going to age out of the system in another couple of years. She'll do better if she has some family ties, however rickety. While her father has had a lot of drug issues, there's no history of abuse between him and Eloise. His demons have always been his own. It's significant that he's reached out to her twice now. It shows a genuine sense of com-mitment to her.'

'Where does he live?' I asked.

'That's the one problem. He's in Powys, which means, of course, Eloise will be a long way away.'

This would be the equivalent of moving across state lines in the US. It meant not only would Meleri cease to be Eloise's social worker, her case would be transferred completely out of the area to a distant part of Wales.

'Does Eloise know?'

'She's been in phone contact with him for a while now, but she doesn't know that he wants her to come live with him. We asked him not to bring this up yet, to give their relationship some time to grow, particularly as she still has time left at Cae Newydd.'

'May I talk about it with her?' I asked.

Meleri nodded.

Eloise was waiting in the beanbag corner when I arrived the next Thursday. Lounged in a very relaxed pose, she balanced the journal on her knee.

'I didn't do this,' she said, a cheeky smile crossing her lips.

I raised my eyebrows in a not-surprised way and sat down.

'Don't you ever get tired of coming here?' she asked.

'Don't you ever get tired of thinking up ways to not do that journal?'

Eloise laughed. I smiled.

'So, if you decided we weren't going to do the journal today, what shall we do?' I asked.

She shrugged. There was a cockiness in her attitude that I

found unexpectedly endearing. 'We could play computer games,' she said. 'We have an Xbox here and we all get to have a go on it, if we earn our points. I have. I got to play a new game this weekend.'

'Uh, no. Nice try, but no.'

Eloise lolled back on the beanbag. There had been plenty of previous occasions when she'd refused to comply with what I'd wanted to do, and we'd had to adapt our sessions to her behaviour, but most of those had been governed by complex emotions. This was the first time she was just being awkward for the sake of it, and it was clear she was relishing this new sense of control. I wanted to validate her assertiveness, but I didn't want to lose track of the session entirely, so I said, 'If we're not doing the journal, why don't you talk to me about your dad. Mrs Thomas told me that he has been ringing you regularly for a while now.'

'Yeah.' She was trying to balance the pen that she normally used for the journal on the tip of her index finger.

'And . . . ?' I asked.

'What do you want me to say?'

'I'm curious what you think about it.'

'He remarried. He didn't even tell me.'

'How do you feel about that?'

She shrugged. 'Pissed off, to be honest. I mean, I'm his daughter. Now I've got a stepmother and I didn't even know it. I hadn't even realized he was out of prison. He never told me at the time.'

'I can see how that would feel upsetting.'

'It's not "upsetting". I know my dad, so I know better than to get upset at the jerky stuff he does, because, like, he's got an addiction and that's a disease. No point feeling upset because someone's doing something you can't control.'

'Yes, you're right.'

'That's what Michael told us in group.'

I nodded. 'Good on Michael, because that's exactly right. And good on you for taking it on board. It's an important insight.'

'I'm still pissed off, though. I said to my dad, "How nice, but I wish you'd told me you were getting married." Because, like, maybe I'd want to come, hey? Maybe I'd like to be there when I was getting a new stepmother. And he's like, "Yeah, I'm sorry, but I didn't know if you could get away from up there." And I'm, like, fuck, you didn't ask. And he's, like, "Never mind, you'll like her a lot, and by the way, you've got a brother." And I say, *a brother!* And I'm, like, really pissed off then, because he never even told me she was pregnant. He didn't tell me any of this stuff until, like, about a month ago, and the baby is already thirteen months old. Don't you think that's foul?'

'Yes, I expect I'd feel angry too,' I said.

She humphed into indignant silence.

Silence pooled around us. Eloise continued to fiddle with the pen for several more moments, but when I didn't speak she flipped it up, caught it and then set it down on the journal beside her. She looked over, made eye contact briefly, and then looked away again.

She said, 'It's kind of cool thinking there's more than just me again, that I have a proper brother. I get fed up having to call every other poor idiot kid in the system who happens to live in the same house as me my "brother". They're not. "Brother" means blood.' She paused. 'But I'd like to see him. They named him Rhodri. That's a king's name. *Rhodri Mawr*. Do you know about Rhodri Mawr? He was king of Wales – of all the Britons – once, a long time ago.'

'That's a good, strong name,' I said.

'Better than "Eloise". "Eloise" doesn't mean anything. I looked it up in a baby book once, and they can't even decide if it's French or German. It might be "Elwigis" or something horrid like that, but then the French got hold of it and named some knight's wife that, or something like that, but, like, nobody knows. Certainly it's not a queen's name.'

'You wish it were?'

'Wouldn't you?' she asked derisively. 'I said that to my dad. I said, why does the baby get Rhodri and I got some crap name no one even knows the meaning of? He said it wasn't up to him what my name was. My mum named me. He said he wanted to call me Angharad, and that is a queen's name. Angharad.' She rolled the name around in her mouth. 'But my mum told him no one would be able to pronounce it. Bitch. It's not that hard. Even I can say it. Angharad.'

I nodded.

'Dad's new wife is named Elen. She's got black hair. He sent me a picture. Elen runs a cafe. That's how he met her. He was going to the cafe to use the internet. Dad said maybe I could work there during the summer break sometime. He said I could earn money.'

'That sounds interesting,' I said. 'What do you think about it?'

She shrugged. 'Like someone's telling me stories.'

'You don't think he'll follow through?'

'No. Because, like, I know how this stuff goes. Dad says, "This time I'm clean and we're going to do this and this and this," but then someone offers him junk and he's off with the fairies. This is what happened last time and the other time and practically every time since before I was born. It's actually amazing he could fit fucking my mother in, because he's been in prison so many times.'

'People can change, you know. It's very hard to do when it comes to things like addictions, which is why slip-ups happen. We get used to certain patterns of behaviour when coping with problems, so it can take quite a few tries to change. But it *can* happen. "Very hard" isn't the same as impossible.'

'Yeah, in the fairy tales,' Eloise replied knowingly.

A silence fell between us. While she was still leaning back in a relaxed manner on the beanbag, her earlier cheekiness had waned. Eloise looked upward, her gaze unfocused. 'It's not just knowing that my dad is going to fail,' she said pensively. 'It's also knowing that if I lived down in deepest rural Powys, I wouldn't be able to talk to anybody, because they'd all speak Welsh. My dad would see to that. He'll be in the Welshest Welsh place he can find. He said they're raising Rhodri first-language Welsh, so I wouldn't even be able to talk to him.'

'I expect Rhodri would be quite happy with your Welsh. Or your English, for that matter.'

'Yeah, but. And see, this is where it matters that I don't even have a Welsh name. If I had a Welsh name I might be okay, because the people around there would know I was Welsh anyway, even if I didn't speak it very well, but instead they'll think I'm English and be horrid to me.'

'I'm sure that's not true of everyone. Yes, some people are jerks, because some people are. But some will be nice. Some will be understanding. There are good people and bad people wherever you go, whatever language you speak.'

She looked over. 'Do you know anything about deed poll? Because I'm thinking maybe I could change my name by deed poll or something, so that Angharad was really my name. It's not as if my mother would care anyway. I'd do it for my middle name. Eloise Angharad. I think that's nice. Better than the middle name I have now. Lee. Eloise Lee. That's not even a girl's name. Eloise Angharad. I like the sound of that. And then, like, if I did decide to go work in Elen's cafe, they could call me by my middle name while I was there.'

'That's an interesting idea,' I said.

She looked over and smiled slightly. 'It would be cool to start over as someone else. I mean, I'd still be me, because I know very well that you can't change things that easily. I'm not so stupid as to think that. But it would be nice to take a break from being Eloise.'

chapter twenty-six

The following week was school mid-term break. My family and I had a holiday in Berlin planned, so I didn't see Eloise. She knew ahead of time about this, of course. I'd explained that I would be away and, consequently, miss our next meeting, but she'd been in such a breezy mood that I wasn't all that sure she had taken the news on board. I was braced for upset when I returned the following Thursday.

It didn't happen. Eloise waved cheerily when she saw me enter the large common room. 'I got your postcard,' she called to me as I crossed the room. 'I put it up on my wall.' As I reached the beanbags, she handed me a mug. 'Here. I made us tea.'

As we settled into our seats and sipped the tea, Eloise continued to chat pleasantly about the things that had gone on in the intervening fortnight. There had been an outing to play ten-pin bowling that she'd particularly enjoyed. Someone had accidentally set off the fire alarm and two fire engines showed up. A new girl had arrived, whose name was Catherine, and whose signature move, apparently, was flashing her boobs. Eloise found this very funny.

She had the journal with her, but it had been set on the floor beside her. To be honest, I'd pretty much given up on the journal by this point. On the plus side, Eloise seemed to be benefitting more and more from the group therapy programme. She was now often mentioning insights she'd gained from the sessions, even when these sometimes seemed unwillingly gained. This made it feel less critical that I push forward with the journal as a therapeutic tool, although I was disappointed at how overwhelmingly unsuccessful I'd been with it.

Eloise looked over at me, almost as if she'd sensed what I was thinking. It was a long, appraising look, and then she slowly set her tea down on the floor beside the beanbag. She picked up the journal.

'I've done something different this time,' she said. Opening the journal, she handed it to me.

Two or three pages were covered with disjointed sentences. *'I wanted to know what was going to happen.' 'A large number of people have gone missing.' 'A promise is something you are supposed to keep.'*

I looked up questioningly.

'I didn't do it very good.'

To be honest, I had no idea what she was trying to do because, from what I could tell, the sentences seemed to have no relationship to each other nor to anything we'd previously discussed. I was, however, reluctant to say anything about my confusion because her expression was so expectant. She was smiling slightly.

'Can you tell what I'm doing?'

I smiled sheepishly. 'Not quite.'

'Those are starter sentences.' A pause. 'You know how you told me about your imaginary person?'

'Yes.'

'You told me once that that's how you got to be a writer, that because you had this person in your head and you kept not knowing how to deal with her, you started writing down what your person did. So . . . I thought, I'm going to write about Olivia like that. I'm going to make everything she's done into stories. Maybe I can sell them! Maybe I can be a writer too!'

I smiled. 'There's an idea.'

'So those are starter sentences. That's what all of them are.'

'Ah, I see.'

'Except . . .' Her brow furrowed. 'How do you go on from there? Because I thought up all these ways to start a story . . . Well, actually, I didn't think them up. I got a book from the library that has starter sentences in it. They're supposed to give you inspiration . . . except . . .' She shrugged. 'I don't know where to go from here.'

I was impressed with Eloise's initiative on this and delighted that she was considering transitioning Olivia into a written character. I explained in more detail how the starter sentence was meant to work as a jumping off point, and then you let your imagination fill in what happens next.

Eloise listened intently, her brow furrowing deeper and deeper. 'I don't see how.'

'Take the sentence "I wanted to know what was going to

happen". You start with that, and you think, "Is this Olivia talking?" And ask yourself, so what *is* going to happen next?'

'I dunno.'

'If it's about Olivia, is she thinking this? Is it about something that's going to happen to her?' I asked. 'Or is it you wondering this about yourself and you're going to interact with Olivia. So you want the next sentence and you get that by asking yourself "What happened before?" "Why is she – or you – wondering this?" Then what? Then what? You just keep asking yourself "then what" after each sentence, and the story grows itself.'

Eloise quirked up the corner of her lip on one side. 'My idea was to write a story and have you tell me if it was good or not, but, crap, where do you get all those words? When I ask myself "what next?", it makes my mind go blank. Writing's harder than I thought.'

'That's true of a lot of things. They look easy until you try them.' I grinned. 'But I think you have an excellent idea, because this is a good way to deal with something that's taking over your mind. You can enjoy experiencing Olivia this way, but she won't clutter up your mind quite so much. Writing things down frees up space in your head. More importantly, it helps give you a little distance from it and that makes it less likely you'll accidentally do things you didn't mean to.'

'It might be a good idea, but it's very hard to do. I didn't get anywhere with these sentences. None of them seem to be about Olivia.'

'Let's try a different approach,' I said. 'Instead of trying to create a whole new story from a starter sentence, what if you just begin at the beginning and tell your own story of Olivia? Start with the first time she came to you.'

Eloise looked at me blankly.

'I remember you telling me about the clothes she was wearing. Rolled-up sleeves? A gilet?'

'I dunno.'

Anxiety was raising its ugly head. I was unsure why it was happening now. Was she afraid of failing? Did she feel as if she'd lost control? Had I inadvertently taken over? I didn't know, but I could sense that this idea of writing about Olivia was in danger of going the way of the journal and so many of our other activities, and I knew I needed to back off.

To divert us, I said, 'I can remember the first time Delilah came to me. I was seven and out playing on my own. My house was on the edge of a small town, and there was a big empty field in back that I used to cut through to go down to a bridge over a stream. It was evening and I remember walking through the tall grass of the field, and suddenly there she was. It felt almost as if she were a person right in front of my eyes, because I had such a clear image of her, but I knew she was just something I made up.'

'Wow,' Eloise said under her breath.

'After that, Delilah was always with me every time my mind went quiet, but I was embarrassed for people to know about her. I worried they'd think I was babyish for having a pretend friend. Or that I was lonely. That was a popular belief when I was young: children only ever had imaginary companions because they were lonely and couldn't get proper friends. But I had plenty of proper friends. In fact, they liked playing with Delilah too. There in middle childhood when we all still had our imaginations, I could make her real for them as well.'

Eloise nodded. 'I'm the exact same as you. I don't want people to know about Olivia. I hate when someone talks about her like she's an out-here person, because it sounds as if I'm mental. I know she isn't real. I know she's just in my head.'

'You aren't mental. You're clever and creative.'

'Hah. I'm not clever. I failed my exams.'

'School isn't the only measure of cleverness. There are different kinds, and research tells us that adolescents who have imaginary companions are creative and intelligent. Having an imaginary companion is a useful way to practise being someone else. You learn how to see things from another point of view besides your own. You develop coping skills. You explore new ideas. Because you have Olivia, we know you are one of those adolescents. So you are clever and creative.'

She lowered her head. 'Olivia just gets me in trouble.'

'Yes, she has gone a little rogue in the past,' I said, 'but that happens. And it's not the end of the world.'

Eloise frowned.

'It happened to me too. I had Delilah go a little rogue on occasion. When I was your age, I remember being so overwhelmed with all the characters living in my head that it spilled over into real life more than once. In my case, people didn't think I was mental so much as they thought I was a huge liar. That was because I kept talking about all this stuff in my head as if it were happening to me. I mean, it *was* happening to me, just not in the literal way people expected.'

This amused Eloise. 'Did you get in trouble?'

'Once, when I was thirteen, Delilah went on a skiing trip and got really sunburned from the snow. Do you know about that? How the snow can reflect sunlight and give you a bad sunburn, even though the temperature outside is low? I don't know why that's what I was imagining, but there was my imaginary character having this exciting time skiing and getting sunburned. Of course, I wanted to talk about such an exciting thing, so when I was on the phone with my friends I told them all about it, only I knew they wouldn't be interested if it was Delilah. So instead of Delilah, I said I was the one who'd gone skiing. Of course, I hadn't. We didn't even own a car in those days, so there was no way I could have gone skiing, and, of course, this also meant I didn't have bad sunburn. Then Monday came around and I had to go to school. I was horrified, because I realized everyone would see that I hadn't told the truth. So you know what I did? I smeared some of my mother's lipstick all over my face and arms to make it look like sunburn.'

Eloise found this hilarious. 'You put *lipstick* on your skin?' She hooted with laughter to the point of almost falling off the beanbag. 'You thought that would fool people into thinking you had a sunburn? Lipstick on your skin wouldn't look like sunburn at *all*. You'd look like a clown.'

'Yes, I know that now. And I probably did look like a clown. My friends, however, were as clueless as me, so they initially believed my story. One of my teachers, however, pulled me aside at lunchtime and made me go wash my face.'

Eloise fell about laughing again. 'That's good. That is one good story. What an idiot you were!'

'Indeed. And that's why I'm telling you, because this kind of idiocy goes along with having imaginary friends. You and I, we've got two realities to deal with, whereas the rest of the world only has one. So while we understand why we're doing what we are, other people don't have context for it, so it gets weird. That's what happened with Delilah and me, and I know full well that's what's happened with you and Olivia too.'

Eloise's smile faded.

'And it's okay. Things got messed up. You were trying to do some Olivia stuff in this world, just like I was trying to do with my lipstick. But we can unmess it. That's the point of my telling you all this. It's okay to have this stuff in your head. And it's okay to make mistakes with it, because mistakes happen. But when they do, we have to sort them out. We need to fix what went wrong. We need to make amends, when that's necessary. And then we need to let go of it and move on.'

Eloise didn't respond. She was looking down at her fingers, which she had splayed across her thighs. Letting the silence settle around us, I listened to quiet sounds beginning to fill the vacuum: distant talking, a fan coming on somewhere, the opening and closing of doors.

'I want to be over the thing with Heddwen,' she said softly.

I nodded.

'I told Michael that last week when we were in group. I said

I just want to be done with it. But you know what he told me? He said my going over to Heddwen's was an addiction, where the urge to keep doing it is very strong, where you've got to make the decision yourself to stop, and it's hard because you get tempted.'

Eloise grew tearful. 'I'm sorry, but it makes me cry. Because if it's like my dad's addiction . . . I mean, he can't do it. He keeps saying he's clean, and he lasts, like, six months, but it just goes on forever. He can't get free of it. Is that going to be me too? I feel like now I've got this flaw in me, that even if I want it to be over I'm always going to be falling back into it, just like my dad does with his junk.'

'Sweetie, I don't think that's quite what Michael meant to say. You don't have an addiction. You are no more addicted to Heddwen Powell than I was addicted to lipstick,' I said. 'Michael was using that as an analogy. He meant that it will be a challenge in the beginning to put yourself on the right track, not because you have inherited your father's addiction, but because all change is challenging. There will inevitably be times when you'll think about going to the Powells', but when that happens there will be ways to cope with the thoughts. What are some examples? What could you do, once you're out and settled back in your foster home, and thoughts of Heddwen occur?'

'I don't know.'

'Well, for example, you could distract yourself. You get the thought about Heddwen, and you think, "That's not helpful. How can I take my mind off it?" Perhaps you could play a computer game instead. Or read a book. Or watch something enjoyable on telly. All those things will change your thoughts, because they make you focus on something else.'

'Michael says I should think about how Heddwen feels. Because she doesn't like it,' Eloise replied.

'That's a good idea too. Trying to see the situation from Heddwen's point of view is very helpful. You might also bring Olivia into those thoughts,' I said. 'Remind yourself of the fact that Heddwen and Olivia aren't the same person. Even though Heddwen gives you good feelings when you are near her, it has nothing to do with Heddwen. You feel good because she personifies Olivia for you. That's the connection you want to break. Get her straight in your mind as a real girl, who feels upset when you bother her.'

Eloise grimaced.

'If you're having trouble with that, remember my lipstick story. Think, "If I impose Olivia things on Heddwen, it's the same as that time Torey imposed Delilah's sunburn on her friends. That got embarrassing because it wasn't true, and this will get embarrassing because Heddwen isn't really Olivia. I don't want to be embarrassed and I will be if I carry on." Do that whenever you think of Heddwen and, I promise you, the feelings will stop.'

'The thing is, they've stopped already. I keep saying that to people, but nobody believes me. I already am embarrassed. I don't want to see her ever again.'

'Then there you are. The change is already underway.'

chapter twenty-seven

Late autumn was upon us with a long string of dark, damp, dreary days when the mist never lifted enough to see the hills, much less the mountains. I made the mistake of complaining to my husband about the weather, muttering something about wishing that if it was going to rain, it would rain properly, instead of day after day of grey skies and the wet fog we called 'mizzle'. This tempted fate and three days of an unrelenting downpour followed, flooding the roads.

I had not resumed the enrichment group in Pen-y-Garth after the summer, so I'd not had occasion to drive again on the road Eloise and I had taken for so many weeks. One November afternoon, however, I had to circumvent the floods in the valley, so found myself coming up over the hill where Eloise and I had always enjoyed the wonderful view of the mountains. The road then descended into Pen-y-Garth. My first thought on entering the village was about the whole debacle with Ffion and Buddug. I wondered how the children were all getting on these days. Craning my neck, I scanned the old school building as I passed. It was mid-morning, so the preschool playgroup was there. Lights were on because of the dull day and I could see little heads bobbing about.

An odd feeling, a mix of regret and nostalgia, filled me. I wished there could have been a better resolution to what had happened, that it would have been possible to know for certain who had been telling the truth, that there would have been some way to revisit the events and set them right. A different track of my mind was paying more attention to what I was feeling as I thought these things. Was there a name for that emotion, that sorrow for unresolved things past? This made me think of Eloise's list of emotions, her momentary fixation with the 'emotion game'. Here was another one that needed to be added to the list.

When I arrived on Thursday to see Eloise, our beanbag corner was empty. I cast around the large community room in case she was off making tea, but I didn't see any sign of her, so I went over to the staff station.

Iain was behind the window. When he saw me, he came out around the desk to talk. 'She's having a bad week,' he said. He then told me that on Monday, when Eloise was coming back from school, she started to choke. She was on the school bus at the time and couldn't catch her breath. The bus driver, fearing she was having an asthma attack or something similar and not knowing what else to do, drove the bus to the A&E department, where Eloise, still choking and struggling to breathe, was taken in for treatment. She was there almost two hours. The final diagnosis: panic attack.

I was surprised at this. Iain's description of what happened sounded both serious and scary, and I wasn't aware of Eloise previously suffering panic attacks. Iain assured me, however, that further investigation at the hospital had shown no evidence of inhalation, asthma or other problems, and Valium had resolved it. Unfortunately, he said, it hadn't ended there. Eloise had had three further panic attacks since, convinced each time that she was choking, going to be sick, going to die. The last one had been just an hour before I arrived, and as a consequence she'd been given Valium and was now having some private time in the quiet suite.

I walked down the corridor to find her, sitting at the same table we'd used on previous occasions after she'd come out of lockdown. There was an opened pot of yogurt and a mug of tea in front of her.

'Hiya,' I said. I looked around the small room.

'Did they tell you what happened?' Eloise asked.

'Yes, and I'm sorry to hear that. It sounded very scary.'

Tears filled her eyes. 'I don't know what's wrong with me. I'm frightened to go to school. I'm scared it's going to happen again.'

I sat down across from her.

She wiped her eyes. 'I feel like I'm going to die. My throat closes up and I start to choke. I think I'm allergic to the fumes on the school bus. I can smell them coming in when the doors open, and I start to choke.'

'Okay, hold on,' I said, and reached across the table to take her hands. 'Did the doctor talk to you about this? Or Michael? Or Iain? Did they explain what's happening to your body?'

'They don't *understand*. It's not in my head. I'm not *mental*. It's real. I get on the bus and start to choke when I smell the fumes. It's *real*.'

'Yes, your feelings definitely are real. I hear what you're saying, but let's see what we can do about it, because they aren't very pleasant feelings. Take a deep breath.'

Tearfully, she looked over at me.

'Take a deep breath,' I said. I got up from my chair and came around behind her. 'Put one hand there, on your chest,' I said, lifting her right hand and setting it just below her throat. 'See how fast you're breathing? That's called "shallow breathing" and, when you breathe like that, it causes your brain to release chemicals that make you feel afraid. So we want to do a little bio hack here. Put your left hand down here, on your tummy.' I moved this hand to the right place. 'Now, I'm going to count to eight, and I want you to breathe in as long as I'm counting, then hold while I count to eight again, and then let it out to the third count. See if you can do it in a way that makes your tummy go out as you breathe in instead of up here on your chest.'

Eloise hesitated.

'*Do it.*'

For once, she didn't resist. I put my hands over hers and we breathed together as I counted slowly – in, hold, out, hold, in, hold, out – for a couple of minutes. Somewhat reluctantly, she began to relax.

'You know where I was this morning?' I asked, as I continued to keep my hands over hers as she breathed. 'Pen-y-Garth. I was just driving through. I'd taken the road to avoid the floods, but it reminded me of our time there.'

'Did you see anyone?'

'No, I didn't stop. But I passed the school. The playgroup was on. I didn't see anyone we knew.'

'I still think about the kids sometimes,' Eloise said quietly. There was a long pause, and then she said, 'I wish I was still in those times. I wish we were still going there. Even if it got messed up at the end, I liked going there.'

'Yes, we had some good fun,' I said.

'I wish I'd known they were good times when I was having them.'

'There'll be other good times.'

Eloise sighed.

Taking my hands off hers, I returned to the other side of the table and sat down again.

Eloise lowered her head. Picking up a spoon, she put it into the yogurt pot. The container was mostly empty, so the weight of the spoon tipped it over. She righted it, took the spoon out and licked it clean before setting it on the table. 'They gave me this because I keep getting a lump in my throat when I eat,' she said. 'Something's wrong, but they don't believe me. I'm scared it's going to happen again. And people are going to laugh at me and not believe me.'

'Iain tells me the doctors looked you over very carefully when you were at A&E and there isn't anything seriously wrong. That's good news, but it doesn't mean what you're feeling isn't real. Panic attacks are a real thing. And they're scary and unpleasant. What it does mean, however, is that they won't actually hurt you. And you can get better from them.'

'I feel like I'm going to die.'

'Yes, they cause awful feelings, but your body's telling you porkies. You aren't going to die. So you need to hang in there until the feelings pass. Awful as they are, panic attacks don't usually last very long. Your body will soon get tired and stop. So you want to remind yourself it's going to pass before too long and you'll be okay.'

'You sound like Michael,' she said. 'He keeps telling me to challenge my thoughts and not be so negative. I'm supposed to say, "Nobody's ever died of a panic attack. So what's the worst thing that will happen?"'

'Yup. Michael's right. It sounds like he's got a good handle on the situation and knows how to help you get past this.'

Eloise sighed heavily. Crossing her arms on the table, she leaned forward, putting her head down on them. 'Everything's so hard.'

I reached out and touched her head.

Two or three minutes passed in silence. As was my habit when things went quiet, I listened into it, mostly as a way of centring myself, but also just to know what else was going on around me. The quiet suite, however, seemed to be soundproofed in some way, because the silence was remarkably complete here. Other than the faint hum of the small fridge nearby, there were no other sounds at all. This, in itself, was calming.

'I'm worried I'm not going to be able to go to my dad's,' Eloise said very softly.

'When is this?' I asked.

'At Christmas. He said I could come spend Christmas with him and Elen and the baby.'

'That sounds nice. Are you looking forward to it?'

She nodded. 'But I have to take the bus down. It's, like, a four-hour journey.'

'Ah,' I said, 'and now you are worried you may have a panic attack on the bus?'

She nodded again.

'When did your dad invite you?'

'Last week. He's been talking for a while about how maybe I could come visit him. Last week he asked if I wanted to come for Christmas.'

'How do you feel about that?'

'Great,' she said. Her voice sounded like it was a fantastic idea, but her posture didn't. She still had her head down, resting on her folded arms in a tired, almost depressed way.

'And maybe you're feeling a little nervous too?'

'No, I want to go. I really do. I'd like to see him.' She straightened up in the chair. 'And I'd like to be out of here, that's for sure. Who'd want to spend Christmas in this place?'

'What's Mrs Thomas said about it?' I asked.

'She's okay with it. My dad's even been saying maybe I could come live with him, if things work out. That's what this is going to be. A trial run. That's what my dad's calling it. If I go and I don't mess up . . . and *he* doesn't mess up . . . and I like it, and he likes it, and Elen likes it too, if we all like it, then maybe I could go live with them. Mrs Thomas talked to me about it last

Sunday. She stopped by, because my dad had been phoning and she knew he'd asked me. And she said, if I wanted to, if I liked it there with him, I could maybe go for real. She said it was possible.'

'Wow, that's a lot of exciting news. How do you feel about doing something like that?' I asked.

'Okay,' she replied and gave a slight, almost disinterested shrug.

'I'm not hearing okay in your body language,' I said. 'I'm hearing "Not so sure".'

'It's mostly that I don't want to get my hopes up too much, because . . .' she rolled her eyes and grimaced, 'who knows what will go wrong.'

A little pause came into the conversation. Eloise picked up the yogurt tub and peered into it. With one finger, she scooped out what remained and put it in her mouth.

'So, let me get this straight,' I said. 'At the end of last week, your dad asked you if you would like to get on a bus and come visit him for Christmas. On Sunday, Mrs Thomas told you that that was all right and that going at Christmas might be a trial run for going to live with your dad permanently. Then, on Monday, you had a panic attack. About riding on buses.'

'Yeah.'

'Do you think there's a connection?'

'What do you mean?'

'Just what I said,' I replied.

She paused, regarding me, her expression perplexed. A moment or so passed, and then her expression slowly changed as the connection occurred to her. Then she wrinkled her nose in scepticism and shook her head. 'No, I don't think so. That would be stupid. No. No, Michael says I just have to stop thinking catastrophic thoughts. I have to let go of wanting things to be perfect.'

'How does it feel, thinking about going to live with your dad?'

'Michael says I've got to stop the panic attacks by not thinking they're going to happen every time I get on the bus. He says to remember all the other times I got on buses and was just fine. That's what I'm going to do.'

'It's all right to be afraid, Eloise. Michael is giving you some good advice and those are useful tools for dealing with panic attacks, but there is nothing wrong with having the feelings you're having. That's a big change, going from here to visiting your dad, much less possibly living with your dad. It's all right to feel scared about that. It's all right to acknowledge you're feeling scared. It doesn't mean you're not happy your dad has asked you, or grateful for this chance, or any of those things. And it certainly doesn't mean you will feel scared forever. It's all right to have the feelings you're having.'

Eloise started to cry. Leaning forward, she covered her face and wept.

'Do you *want* to go to your dad's?' I asked, as the tears began to subside. 'I mean, *really* go? Because it's also all right not to want that. It *is* a big change, and I'm sure we don't know all the history with your dad that you know. So please do realize that it's all right to say to Iain and Michael and Mrs Thomas that you don't want to go, if you don't.'

'I *do* want to go. That's the thing. I *do* want it. So much that I can't even say how much.'

'And just feeling a bit overwhelmed by it all?'

She nodded. 'Yeah.'

'That's okay. You'll be okay.'

She nodded again. 'Yes, I know I will.'

And so it was. I saw Eloise on two more Thursday afternoons. The meetings were pleasant and largely mundane. During this period she had two further panic attacks, neither of which were as bad as the first ones. We talked a bit about them, but for the most part I left that up to Michael and the group therapy sessions. Instead, Eloise and I talked about girlie things, about procuring the kind of make-up she liked, about what she wanted to wear on the visit, and what she should do about gifts.

And then it was the end. During the last half hour of our last session together, Eloise took me down to her room, because she wanted to show me the gifts she'd chosen for her father, Elen and the baby. Afterwards, she walked with me to the front door as I prepared to leave.

'*Nadolig llawn*,' she said at the door and smiled. 'I'm going to say that to my dad when I get off the bus. He'll be pleased.'

I grinned. 'I think you'll want to say *Nadolig llawen*. Because otherwise, instead of wishing him Happy Christmas, you'll be wishing him a full Christmas. Although after looking at that big box of chocolates you're bringing him, a "full Christmas" might be true enough.'

Eloise laughed at her mistake. 'I'll tell him an American told me how to speak Welsh.'

Suddenly a stricken look crossed her face. 'What if this is the last time I ever see you?'

'I'm sure it won't be. Bye now. Safe travels. And *Nadolig llawen*.'

'*Nadolig llawen* to you too.'

epilogue

In the vast majority of cases I do not see children again. Despite how intense and meaningful our relationship may be during our time together, once it is over they move on to the next stage of their lives and seldom look back. This is both normal and healthy.

So it was with Eloise. Christmas came, and she left to visit her father and his new family. Meleri told me that the visit went well. As we both anticipated, Eloise chose to stay, and that was the last I heard of her. I hoped, of course, that everything worked out, but all I knew for certain was that she never returned to the care system in our county.

The advent of social media has changed the way we relate with people from our past, particularly those who were with us for a season or two and then moved on. These days peers from primary school, old university buddies and long-ago work colleagues reincarnate on our screens as 'Someone You May Know', and countless reconnections are made with people who, in previous generations, we would have lost all contact with.

Fifteen years after Eloise and I had parted on that December afternoon, I received a Facebook message from someone with a screen name I didn't recognize. When I opened it, it said simply: 'It's me. Eloise.'

She was delighted to find me and quick to explain that I wouldn't have found her, because, as she had foretold those many years back, she was now Angharad. Did I remember that conversation? she asked. Did I recall that she was going to add Angharad as a middle name? In the end, she chose Angharad as her first name and Eloise was now her middle name. Official too, she said, changed by deed poll when she was eighteen.

Eloise was eager to catch up. How were things? Where was I? What was I doing? she asked in quick succession. I told her that I was still writing, still working with kids, but not with the same charity. My husband and I had split, and I was no longer living in Wales.

She was still in Powys. She'd had what she described as 'an interesting few years' after we'd parted. Things hadn't worked out with her dad. Several rolling eye emojis came up on the screen. As if we'd believed they would, she added. He was a 'good guy', she said, but his demons were too strong. Before her first year in Powys had passed, he'd fallen victim to his addiction again. Caught burgling houses for drug money, he was sent back to prison. Two years later and still in prison, he died of a heart attack.

'It could have all ended there, like a bad novel,' she wrote, 'except for Elen.' Her father's second wife was only ten years older than Eloise, more a sister than a mother, and she had been kind and nurturing from the start, putting up with Eloise's first rocky months, making her feel welcome, and always fostering the relationship between her and her baby brother, Rhodri. Although Elen and Eloise's father divorced, Elen made it clear that the divorce didn't extend to Eloise and invited her to stay on. She gave Eloise that promised job in the cafe and encouraged her to continue in education. For the first time, Eloise enjoyed the stability and support she had never experienced from her own family.

I was enjoying our conversation on Messenger, but it was stilted. 'I'm afraid I still write like shit,' Eloise complained. 'There's so much I want to tell you, but I can't express anything properly this way.' She asked if there was any chance we could meet up at some point and 'have a cup of tea for old days' sake'. I wasn't very often in the area, but I said yes, the next time I was through, we would.

If I'd passed her on the street, I wouldn't have recognized grown-up Eloise. She had slimmed down. Her adolescent skin had cleared. Her hair was now cut in a short, wavy, 1920s bob and tastefully highlighted. Her make-up was a bit dramatic, but stylish. Her clothes were vintage cool. And in a pushchair beside her was a baby, perhaps eighteen months old, sleeping peacefully.

Eloise greeted me fulsomely, hugging me tightly. As we came apart, she nodded towards the pushchair. 'That's Owain. He's mine.'

'He's bonny,' I said.

She nodded. 'He is. He's also asleep, so come on. Let's go in, before he realizes what he's missing. Tell me about yourself. Tell me everything.'

In the small cafe, we ordered pots of Earl Grey tea, and, because this was my first time back in Wales in quite some time, bara brith. Eloise was animated in her conversation, full of an enthusiasm I didn't remember her having in her teens, which made me wonder how depressed she must have been during those years.

'Did I tell you about my work?' she asked. 'I'm a graphic designer these days. Did I tell you I went to college? I don't know why school was so hard for me when I was a kid. Like, I went there about three hours a week when you and I were seeing each other. I just couldn't get my head around it in those years. I think it was being with Dad that changed me, seeing what a hot mess he made of his life, even though he was such a good guy at heart. And I guess I was getting old enough not to be so stupid, because instead of wanting to run away, seeing him made me want to sort myself out. That, and Elen. Elen has helped me so much. We had computers in the cafe, and she was always asking me to make stuff for her. Create a flyer for this, put a poster in the window for that, make the menus pop. She could tell I was able to do stuff and she gave me the opportunity to do it. It just carried on from there.'

Eloise paused. 'I brought you something. Hang on a sec. Because I wanted you to have this to remember me by.' Opening the big handbag she was carrying, Eloise pulled out a folder and removed several papers. Each was a slickly designed graphic of an attractive dark-haired woman in different, dynamic poses. They looked like advertisements for an action film.

'These are good,' I said, because they genuinely were, although I couldn't quite tell what they were for. There was no text on them.

Eloise smiled. 'Guess who it is.'

'No idea,' I said.

'That's Olivia. Remember how you were always wanting me to write about her? But I couldn't. That's because I'm not a writer. It took me a while to realize that. But then I also realized I wanted to express her visually, because that's more the way I think, but I'm not an artist either. So when I started my design course, this was one of the first things I did. To be honest, I kind of did it for you, even though you weren't around any longer.'

'That is cool,' I said, and smiled.

'That was the best part about you and me,' Eloise replied, 'that you let me talk about Olivia, that it was okay that I told you all the daft stories I would make up about her. You *understood*. I can still remember that first time when you told me that you'd had something like that in your head too and you didn't act like I was away with the fairies.'

I picked up the pictures again and studied them.

'If she looks familiar, it's because she's based on the lady who stars in *SVU: Special Victims Unit*,' Eloise said. 'It's her photos I started with.'

'Yes, I thought I recognized her,' I replied.

'Do you remember once you asked about Olivia? You asked if I could remember when she first appeared to me? At the time,

I said something about not knowing, but the truth is, I did know. I was just embarrassed to tell you that she was nothing more than a character off the telly,' Eloise said. 'She was Olivia Benson. That's where the name came from. I was seven or eight and living with my mum and Darren at the time. I used to watch *SVU* every single night on one of those repeat channels, while waiting for Darren to bring home a takeaway. It was always, like, after he'd been to the pub and I was so sleepy I couldn't sit up at the table. All I really remember was sitting in front of the telly, hungry and waiting, and I think I sort of fell in love with Olivia Benson. Darren would do his stuff to me, and afterwards I'd imagine Olivia Benson coming and talking to me. Coming to take care of me.'

'Okay, yes, that character is a very understandable choice,' I said.

'My Olivia took on a life of her own after a while. She got younger in my imagination. By the time I was with you, she was, like, seventeen and went to secondary school, because then I could have school adventures with her that reflected better what I was experiencing myself. But then . . .' Eloise gave a rueful smile. 'Then all that daft business with Heddwen Powell happened.' She blushed. 'I mean, that mortifies me even to this day. To be truthful, I've wanted to look you up before now, but it's taken me this long not to be too embarrassed to see you.'

I shrugged. 'It was what it was at the time. We all do daft things in our teens.'

'Heddwen was as if Olivia had come to life. It's hard to explain what that felt like, but, well, it made me a bit nuts. It was an obsession. It really was. I can remember how alive I felt around Heddwen, but I knew it was wrong too, and I couldn't stop it. I couldn't stop myself. It was a relief in many ways, going to my dad's that Christmas, because it was so far away. To be honest, I think that was a large part of why I wanted to stay. It was the only way I was able to escape what Heddwen was doing to my head. God, those years. Thank goodness they are behind me!'

I smiled.

'But Olivia stayed. I lost Heddwen, but Olivia was still with me. I remember you telling me once about how you had a hard time as a kid, and what made your imaginary person so important was that no one could take her away from you. I've thought about that so many times. I've used it as a kind of talisman, that knowledge no one could take Olivia away from me. They got everything else. My mother. My home. My sister and brother. Even my father, bless him. But Olivia was mine.' Eloise laughed. 'Remember how I always used to make up all those dramatic stories about her? Like, she was in a car crash one minute and falling off a cliff the next minute?'

I laughed too. 'Yes, I definitely do.'

'Mostly I just had a dramatic turn of mind. Those were weird years because, on one hand, they were quite harrowing, but on the other, to be honest, they were deadly boring. I always wanted more excitement, and I could get it with Olivia. But I also think part of it was because I *knew* she was safe. That no matter what, you're never going to lose that person in your head. Which was good, because knowing I could love Olivia and not lose her made me brave enough to try loving real people.'

Smiling, I nodded.

We paused over our tea. Eloise leaned down to check on Owain, who slept on.

'Is Olivia still with you?' I asked.

She shook her head. 'That's the irony. She's pretty much gone these days. Every once in a while, something will happen to make me think about her again, but she's not in my head in the same way as she used to be. It's been five or six years now since she was a big part of my life.' Eloise paused. 'After what I just said, you'd think that would feel catastrophic, but it doesn't. Olivia faded naturally, and she just feels like a good memory these days. I get a bit nostalgic occasionally, because she was such an important part of my life for so long, but not sad.' She smiled. 'But saying that, I've enjoyed getting these old graphics out,' she said, tapping the papers she'd given me. 'It's reminded me of how much I loved her. And how much I've wanted to share this with you.'

The baby stirred and opened his eyes. Eloise leaned down. 'Hello, *cariad*, did you have a good sleep?' She unbuckled the pushchair harness and lifted him up into her lap.

'Motherhood was a bit of a surprise,' she said to me. 'His dad and I . . . it was always casual between us. He's a good bloke, but we aren't really in a relationship. Darren pretty much fucked up my interest in that. And I never once pictured myself with a kid. You know what I mean? I was going to be footloose and fancy-free, mostly because I was determined not to fuck someone up the way my parents did me. I always felt it was selfish to have a child, because he doesn't ask to be born, he doesn't get any say in whether or not he wants to cope with this world. That's what I always believed, but sometimes life has its own surprises in store.'

She smoothed the baby's hair and kissed him just above his ear. 'I just look at him, and I think, how did I get so lucky? How did I get this chance? Hey, *cariad*? How did I get so lucky to have you?' She kissed him again.

The baby squirmed and reached for the table.

'*Wyt ti eisiau bisged, cariad*?' Eloise said. Opening her bag, she took out a chocolate-covered digestive biscuit, broke it in half. '*T'eisiau bisged? Bisged?*' She handed it to the child. '*Ta?*'

'*Ta,*' the baby said.

Over his head, Eloise grinned at me. 'I know. I was the one who was never going to speak Welsh. But things change. Elen is first-language Welsh, and she spoke it all the time with Rhodri. No one was fussed if I did or not, but I'm proud of it now, and I want Owain to be first-language. He's got a proper king's name, you know. Owain Glyndwr. I want him to be proud of who he is. I want him to know where his roots are. I want him to *be* someone.'

There was a small pause.

'That doesn't sound quite right,' Eloise added. 'I don't mean someone, as in someone rich or famous. I couldn't care less about that. What I mean is someone who is important to himself.'

She reached over for the teapot and poured the remainder

between our two cups. 'When I tell people about what I came out of, and how my dad was, even after I got here, they ask me what's changed for me. "What did Elen do?" I say she didn't do anything other than be there. That was true for you too, and to be honest, it was true for my dad. People underestimate how powerful that is. They want to know what you *did*. And I say, you showed up. And you cared that I showed up.'

She kissed the baby on the side of his head. 'And that's what I want for him. To feel he matters. To feel he's seen.'

Also by million-copy bestselling author Torey Hayden

Lost Child

The True Story of a Girl who Couldn't Ask for Help

'As sweet as Jessie often was, it was clear that she was a deeply angry young girl who did not yet have a productive means of expressing all of what was going on inside.'

Jessie is nine years old and looks like the perfect little girl, but she also knows how to get her own way and will lie, scream, shout and hurt to get exactly what she wants. Her parents say they can't take her back, and her social workers struggle to deal with her destructive behaviour.

Finally, educational psychologist Torey Hayden is called in to help. Torey's gentle care and attention reveal shocking truths behind Jessie's lies. Can Jessie now accept this first experience of consistent loving care, or will she push it away too?

'Hayden is a fine storyteller, recounting the touching bonds that form among children and between Hayden and her students.' – *Washington Post*

'Torey Hayden deserves the kind of respect I can't give many people. She isn't valuable, she's incredible. The world needs more like Torey Hayden.' – *Boston Globe*

Available now in paperback and eBook.